For Maya

This book is dedicated to YOU, my little mouse.
No other existence or form of life or anything else
in this world has ever changed my little box as
much as YOU have.
If I chose to or not, YOU have given me no other
chance than to constantly reflect upon myself,
change myself and feel true love for other human
beings, more in my life than ever before. Part of
my own reflection was this book and I'm thankful
that it was written, even though it doesn't mean
much in my own world.

Most things can't be written down or explained, so
I don't even try.

I love you more than I could ever tell you.

The Box I Call Life

Lily Lu
Little Swastika

CONTENTS

PROLOGUE

It has now been 13 years since the inspiration emerged about what life could be. Let's call it enlightenment, awakening or simply put, a change in my way of life. There was something that burned itself into my head and changed my life's foundation completely.

I call this event 'The days my consciousness became conscious'. I will get back to this experience in detail later on. During this time I was living steadfastly in the outside world even though I already knew that I didn't feel comfortable within it or adapt well to it. It was a time in which I was lost within myself and astray in this world.

In that phase, I read a lot of philosophical works and books but all of them seemed useless to me because most of these authors try to push opinions on you, tell you that their way is the one and only. One day a certain book fell into my hands, "Jiddu Krishnamurti – Freedom from the known".

I wouldn't go so far as to say this book changed my life but I will say that it contributed to my curiosity- big time. I began to question everything and built my perspective of the world. I also halted my studies and ceased reading any kind of philosophical, scientific or religious material expressing views on the world. In my opinion, it is wonderful if something triggers your thinking and eventually leads you to find yourself, yet too much outside influence may let you drift away from your initial goals. There is also the implied danger of being trapped in that pattern of the author, simply adapting to that.

From my point of view, it benefits one greatly to

be free from all that and create your idea of life and live it that way.

Over many years I've recommended Krishnamurti's book to a lot of people, telling them how it was the origin for me to change my own life. More precisely, it was why I began to define life by myself, even if my notions contradicted his teachings. Also, it should be made very clear that these events were at least a decade ago and within this passage of time I can't recall it all but this book is positively one of the reasons I made a life out of this human existence. I started questioning my own life and made many tough decisions. Each of them was followed by harsh and strong consequences.

I went on my path from early on with the attitude that I'll do things in exactly the way they feel right for me, and I walk this path, whether it is successful or not. What we see as success is a matter of perception and perspective. For example, if I want to be self-employed and it is an all-time dream of mine, is not the attempt to do it a success in itself? Even when I'm bankrupt the next year, at least I tried. That attempt is more of a success than if I'd never tried at all.

Switching sides, would it be a success working a lifetime with a good position in a 9 to 5 job without any financial plight but therefore never living my dream? Which point of view tells us what success is?

I realized early on that I would rather drown with what I do than waste my life away as a peasant. This is what my life is about. It is how I define life and that is what this book is about. I have been carrying this idea in my head for the last

3

ten years and it took me countless experiences and trips to sort my thoughts, eventually putting them into understandable words because what I define as living life is completely different from how most people would define it. It may be absurd in a way that you might not find any connection to your own life. Maybe it is not. Perhaps there will be an approach, a development, revealing actual connecting points. Who knows? Everybody has his reality. At least you should have one or try to find it.

Am I stupid enough to know that I`m a wise man or am I wise enough to know that I don't know anything at all?

I neither perceive myself as a spiritual person nor as an erudite human. I rather see myself as a silly and naive man who is clueless about what's going on in the outside world. It has been quite a while since I released myself from the idea that any knowledge of humanity will get me further ahead on my path. Even this book is just another work of a human, and this being said, it should be seen as completely non-trivial because this is my view, my world, and my reality. I guess in not one moment is it matching anyone else's perception. Everybody has to define life by him or herself.

That's what this book is about, respectively, my view on life. What is life? That is a question I ask myself every day, nevertheless, it's a question that will keep me occupied for the duration of my existence.

To define life is a more complex task than one would think, especially in which many-folded ways the outside world interacts with your mind and vice versa, most of all how much my mind is influenced by outside circumstances. If I want to define my own life, don't I have to start by first defining myself?

I don't see myself as a philosopher, teacher, shaman or someone that tries to lead or influence others. I love confrontations and I rather see myself as someone who confronts people with (their) life as many are keeping up a masquerade for our society without admitting it, not even to themselves. Even if they do admit to this charade - Do they have the guts or even the mental energy to release themselves from it, especially when they lead a simple and good life?

I see myself as someone who questions everything and everyone, curious about any kind of reality. I even love to discuss with people who share my opinion just to find out why exactly they have this viewpoint. It's not only with others; I'm questioning myself the most.

The people that know my work and know me are aware of how many fences I've jumped and how many boundaries I've broken within my rituals and experiences. Everything I do is connected to what is happening in my head.

Borders have to be crossed mentally first. No matter in what form or respect, this border crossing will adapt in your life later on. Even if it takes a lot of time, energy and passion, what comes out of it is in no relation to the effort.

It took my life and existence to become the person I am today. I guess I'm still a great distance away from how I want to see myself and still very far from defining my life as a life worth living.

These two basic things are a big part of my life

5

and have influenced my way of thinking resulting in the way it is today.

1. Rituals in the form of out-of-body experiences

This is something we don't get to know in the world of today anymore. For example, Body Suspensions in which you hang on hooks that have been pierced through your skin or rituals that were used by native tribes and cultures since the dawn of time to mark certain stages of life and/or to assist in spiritual development. These rituals are designed to increase consciousness; some even are actual near-death experiences. I gathered more and more experiences of this kind over the years and traveled the world to participate in the most different kinds of Rituals. I bent and crossed my limits again and again and, in consequence, exposed my body to almost inhumane strains.

These experiences give rise to the question; what are our limitations and what is it doing to us if we manage to transcend them?

2. Psychedelic rituals

These are Rituals during which I consume pure, undiluted substances like Ayahuasca, Mescaline, LSD or DMT to travel into the depths of my mind. I do not consider this consumption as drug abuse as shaman used many of these rituals for thousands of years to help and heal people.

Unfortunately, a lot of this is illegal in the world nowadays and, in most people's heads, equal to drug abuse. However it may be, I crossed a lot of borders during the performance of physical rituals and again found new borders that I crossed ever further. From there I started creating and forming new and adapted rituals.

When I started to work on this book about the aspects of my life I concluded that these two leading aspects would not be a part of this book. They helped a lot to mold my view of life to become the person I am today. Without them my arts and all I do would be non-existent in this form but, in the end, these subjects are just too big to make mention of in my first book.

I am conscious about the fact that exactly these subjects and my experiences around them might be of interest to a lot of people but this is also why I leave them out for now as it would be a shame to just scribble them and not go into depth. I will continue my writing work with separate books about those experiences and enrichments that these subjects contained for me.

This book reflects my idea of what I connect with the words 'to live life' and what it personally means to me being alive. It will explain what there is behind the word that I use in my world and that can be found in nearly all of my arts in some way. It can bring you closer to what I feel living life defines and is. I would be more than happy if my view encourages or stimulates some of you to understand and eventually pull something out of it to change yourself.

Still, the last thing I want is for my view of life to be regarded as the only way or have it impersonated because that is the exact point. Question everything. Doubt! Everything that I don't question or that I don't have doubts about is going to influence my deeds and therefore my life. Without my questioning, there will never be answers and to come to a question, I've got to relieve myself from what is already inside of me.

Also, I won`t say that religion is less realistic than a scientific or philosophic point of view. Everything is possible, can be, and is a reality in its own way for those who truly believe.

There is no such thing as absolute reality and even this book solely contains human words written by a soul who's been shaped by the outside world through and through. It reflects my views according to the actual form, or simply put, to the actual form of my existence in the form of my consciousness. But, as I doubt myself as well and rarely, take myself too seriously, all this means nothing in the end.

As we adapt to change because of outside circumstances, we adapt and change within. We are a new generation of humans and as much as I love the old shamanic rituals, I am aware that they don't help me one bit in modern life if I don't utilize them in a way so they can influence and mold my reality today.

In a very strange way, we are our own creators. Even though our body is in existence, the mind develops later on in life. In most cases though, it is not created by ourselves but by outside influences and events. When the day comes in which we decide to create our self, we create our self, maybe not completely new but partly, as we are the creator of our world, where the body which is the outside vessel reflects the (our!) outside world that we live in.

I am truly aware that my body looks completely different after years of these experiences. Crucial, not only because it is aesthetic in my eyes but also I adapted my ideals of beauty because of this.

In the beginning, I found beauty to distance myself from society's norms about beauty. The years in this body led me to give up any kind of view on beauty at all, and even question that.

If out of a certain reason, I want a new face, the aesthetic reason is non-relevant and not relative. To take a look in the mirror afterward and be aware that you liked the old face more...oh well, we all don't get to pick our faces, right?

I like to crack jokes about the fact that I am at a point where there is nothing left to rescue but this allows me to do anything, as, from the esthetic point of view, the condition cannot become any worse. My body has been through a lot by jumping the fences of my senses.

Enduring years of the most extreme life of living in my body, it became what it is now. Still, I guess I will never be able to show an outside reflection of how I feel on the inside, how different from most people I met in my life and diverse from how I see this world.

I will try to keep all this plain, simple and understandable, as, in my eyes, it usually doesn't take too many words to put across what I want to put across. When there is a misunderstanding it's mostly out of other reasons than the lack of words.

Even if I am still not understandable in some of my words here and there, I try to describe my views on reality with simple means and examples. Also, I am not a big friend of formal speech and even less of grammar or the rules of orthography. It won't make it easier but if you take a pen and a sheet of paper whilst reading the first chapter and play with it the way I do you can easily comprehend what I mean when I describe things in the way that I do.

The box I call life. I thought about the title a lot, for many years. Yet that is what it is because my vision is not free or unforced. It is just a box among others because, in the end, we all live in our boxes in a kind of imprisonment within ourselves, with our own particular way of thinking and our personal view on what we call life.

To say it clearly once more: When I write about life, I do it in the form of "to live life" and not in the form of the actual life in the shape of human existence because, to live life in the form of existence, you don't need much of a mind and you would need fewer words for sure.

THE BOX

Our box

Small boxes: One of my favorite and most used terms when I talk about life. There seem to be many ways to describe the ways of thinking that we've acquired, to describe masks and patterns which society pushes onto humans from a very early age. It is a box that can be huge, as big as one can imagine but still not as vast as the knowledge and experiences of humans in this world. Even if we think our box is huge, it can still be tiny, even smaller than what we define as very small. From my point of view, I would claim my box is rather small. Tiny. And even if I would read every single book on this planet, I would still have a pretty small box.

Let us take a sheet of paper and draw a box on it. Under the lower side of it, we make a dot, which represents our point of view. I am aware of the fact that everyone would partly or completely have a different point of view about things but let's take this box now and write three words of personal importance into it. What do we see when we look at these words? What meaning do these words have for us? Why exactly did we pick these words? We give ourselves a little time to think about it in depth.

Why do these words mean what they mean to us? Is it really just our imagination or just the idea of what we learned to associate with them? Is it only the meaning that we've had imprinted into our heads? Is it a different idea, thoughts of others; is it something we created in our minds?

Unfortunately, I've got to admit that, for my part, over the years of traveling through my consciousness, all I associate with something was in the same way influenced by something else. Even if these influences hide in the depths of our minds. But to get rid of these associations and their connectedness is, as far as I see it, not possible on an outside-worldly level.

I came to this conclusion about twelve years ago and that's when my box started changing and shape shifting like never before, nor after. Ever since I feel it is my mission, my goal in life and I wrap my existence around it, to get these manifestations of emotions and ideas out of my system again.

I will dig into that later on in detail.

Back to our box.

Let us look at it and the first word in it. In my case, it would most certainly be the word 'life'. In your case, it will likely be a different word but for some reason, this very word, whatever it may be, is not of importance, but why it is there in the first place.

What is our idea of it? What is it we connect with it? Have we ever spent a deeper thought on it or is it just what it is? In which way can we disengage from the influences that we have concerning this word and create a new meaning for it? Is it required to designate this word as a word and is it even possible to find other words for this word?

Let's take this sheet of paper in front of us with the box on it and the dot at the bottom and turn it upside down. Now we'll make a new dot at the bottom of the box and look at that word upside-down.

Even if you can`t read the word anymore, it still has the same meaning, the same meaning in a completely different form. The first dot we drew represents the way we look at things and the way it was taught to us, as well as everything we experienced with it, everything they told us about it, and what we've read or seen. The emotion, association or experience one might have with this word can be absolutely different from what others would associate with it. Languages were designed to give names to certain things or put emotions into words so that mutual understanding and communication became possible. Yet it seems there are limits to it, as otherwise there would not be tons of poems, movies, songs and paraphrases about the word 'love' for instance.

To release yourself from your old points of view and to look at something in a fresh way is one of the most beautiful traits of which humans are capable. This ability is something we have within us from our first day on earth but eventually, education, society, and the indoctrination within our school-systems destroys it.

What happens if we look at this word upside down? I don't mean to see it as a word that is upside down but release yourself from the idea that it is, in fact, an upside-down word. Try to create a new association with what you see. Are we able to do so at all?

Maybe we like our word even more in this way and maybe we can modify the word so that it is appealing from our inverted point of perspective. At least the meaning doesn't change because we know what word we have placed there and what kind of emotion or with which event it is anchored within us.

16

To learn and understand how stuck we are to our viewing point was, and is, the toughest thing for me to realize. And we still are in our box and dealing with our own point?

Can we play with this word? How much can we release ourselves from our individual idea?

Release from the top, bottom, right, left. We can regard this word free from any point of view and it still has the same meaning, yet from the outside, it has a completely d i f f e r e n t expression and optic. And still, we are on the two-dimensional plane, in a two-dimensional box on a sheet of paper.

Now imagine that you let the box wander towards a three-dimensional box to the top. Still,

.THE SNOW BALL THEORY.

EARTH.

your word is in the middle, which you can now see from all the perspectives, mirrored, rotated, viewed from above. See which different kinds of possibilities in which you can now view this word,

17

completely new, although it still has the same meaning and association.

To me, it is not about this word itself or its meaning. It is about the mere imagination that we were once capable of and still are. By 'once' I am referring to the time before we were molded into what to 'think and feel'. The time back when we couldn`t express ourselves through words for emotions or objects that we were eventually given through our language.

We can see the influences if we take a word that is of high importance to us, yet we have never seen it in another way than the way it is written. We were told that this word stands for a certain item or emotion. If you write it upside down it will still be the same word and you are eventually tempted to turn the sheet of paper around instead of taking it 'as is'.

One has an association with the letters, words and the way of writing it as soon as you 'learned' how to use this word 'properly'. It doesn't matter which language it is written in, or if it is a foreign language and/or scripture. There is no 'right' or 'wrong' as we are free from any sort of meaning of what lies in front of us. So if I'm aware of the meaning, is how the word displayed really that important?

I play with these given associations that some have trouble releasing them from in my art and turn around, mirror or cut off words. It doesn't change the meaning but the appearance. It gets unreadable for people that hold on to the 'right' way of writing. The same goes for spelling.

How many hold on to the total orthography and are almost unable to process the context if there is 'something wrong'. If there is one "s" too many or the word is written in paragraphs or not – to me it has the same meaning.

In the German language, some words change their meaning once they are written in paragraphs. There are exceptions and normally you can see its meaning by reading the context of the complete sentence even if the eloquent Germans doubt this, even if they must admit that one can distinguish these words in a pronounced way, although there are no linguistic differences for upper and lower cases in the German language.

Many languages do not use capitalization apart from languages that have a different type of writing system or characters. German is one of the much more complicated languages. Although I doubt that one can express more in German than in any other language. Maybe we are just more caught up in expressing ourselves. And yes, when I use a word such as `life', everyone knows what I mean by that, or not at all since what I once connected with it has nothing to do with what I express with it nowadays.

Get close to the word. So close that you only see a single letter. And now the whole game starts again. From how many points of view can this letter be considered? How far does it change when you walk around, turn it and play with it? If there is no point in your box and you fly around freely, how close can you go? What does the structure of your letter look like? How does it feel?How does it smell? As silly as it sounds, that's how silly it is.

For who tells us how we can or should look at a letter, a word or a whole sentence? I refer the whole thing to pretty much everything that exists. Just as we connect something with a word, we also do it with an object or other things and stop questioning or discovering it.

I love looking at children, how free they look, feel, smell and taste things and how they create their own image. How brutal is it the adult comes, takes it out of their hands and tells them what it is?

Take a stone for example. A child finds a rock for the first time in his life. This stone can be everything or nothing. This stone is completely meaningless and is explored by the child. Sensed, smelled, tasted from every perspective, from near and far. This stone can be anything, a completely new universe, a life, a cosmos, a new world full of beauty and experiences. A child can spend an eternity with this stone and play with it, creating its own image and imagination. It is completely free, uninhibited and limitless in this idea, and I mean limitless.

But then society comes into play in the form of an adult person, teacher or other leading figures, taking the stone out of the child's hands and saying 'this is a stone'.

At that moment, the free idea of what it might be breaks apart from what you make of it yourself. Society says it's a rock so do not question it. It is the day when a stone just became a stone and nothing else.

The positivity of this can now be argued. Some would say that this is what sets us apart from the Stone Age men, who had to learn everything from the beginning and didn't have the opportunity to quickly acquire 'knowledge'. When I'm in countries and places where people live very isolated and 'simple', where people, tribes, and entire villages are so isolated that not much of today's modern world has arrived there, then I have to admit that these people are so much happier and freer than anyone I know in the Western world, like children. Children have significantly less knowledge than most adults and yet are much happier and more at ease living. While the adult loses his laugh, children enjoy the most banal little things, for example; something like a stone.

And these are essentially small experiences, especially in larger terms such as 'life', 'love', 'family', 'work', etc. The impressed manifestations are set clearer and harder. And the more difficult it will be to be able to release yourself from it later in life.

Back to the box. Now if we fly away from very close

to a faraway distance and hold the paper away from us so far that we can only perceive the outlines of the word, a rough abstract form, we can also view and play with this shape from every perspective in our box, from left and right, up and down, near and far. How far are we still capable of our own way of thinking? How far are we still able to reach the limits of what is possible with something as simple as a written word on a piece of paper? And now I ask the question: how freaky is it what we can do with just a simple word without changing the meaning of it? So purely, visually in our mind and only with the shift of our perception and view of what lies ahead, we still only move in the visual perception within our own box.

Whatever you did with your hand or your word, if you put it back in the start position, you will realize that it was just a word, one in three, and only the visual representation of a concept, emotion or experience no matter how many words you fill into this box.

These are only words in a box. The visual perception of what we were taught. As soon as you deviate from this learned and learned template, you will not understand too many people, even though the other representation of a word may describe exactly the same thing as the unified viewpoint.

But how far is the mutual understanding of what you want to express or experience yourself? How far is it necessary to limit your consciousness to better interact with the external world? How far is one able to limit oneself by knowing what one is capable of in one's mind?

Who tells us what reality is and what makes it a reality?

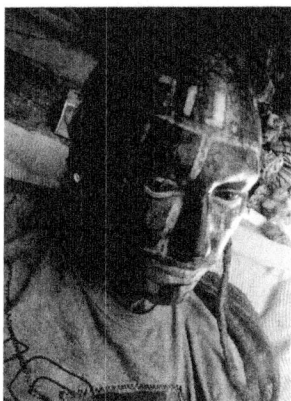

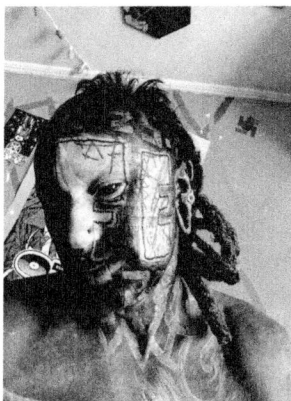

Let's get back to the box and back to our first word. Who tells us when we are at the end of contemplation and imagination? Who tells us when we are in our imagination and have just finished our consciousness? Who? Not me! And even if I am on the edge of what I can achieve in my imagination, it is important to understand, or better accept, that this is only my own limit in which I have come across in the current existence, where it does not continue at the moment. But to speak of a final limit is very far-fetched and not nearly possible in my imagination. I think that I have put down any idea of a limit, any idea that I or other existing life forms have reached a point where their or all my potential is fully exhausted. Even if I do not reach a certain limit for decades and someday recognize and accept it as my ultimate limit, even then, it is not said that it is not a limit that someone else can break or have to accept for their self.

The box. Our word is black on white in front of us. What is black? What is white? It is a gradient of different pigmentation and shades. Yes, black is black in the intention, as we have learned it. But, depending on the light source, depending on the gradient and depending on the view, you can see a completely different color spectrum behind it apart from how each person perceives and looks at different colors. So now we look at our word from this point of view.

We break away from the fact that it is a black word on white paper and rediscover it, staring at the word, or pinching our eyes a little. Change the color in our consciousness and look at the word in a different charisma than black and white.

And other colors have different expressions and any other associations affiliated with them.

Where a blue word or the color blue gives me a rather dark, negative effect, it might have the complete opposite effect on someone else. Behind blue can be in one, the greatest joy and deepest emotions, whereas with someone else this color is negatively affected. Thus, the radiation of a word is differently affected by the color in which it is written, not to mention the color of the background and the interaction between the two colors. How do we ever see colors? I am aware that we see colors differently and also perceive the interaction of colors differently. I believe that this is very much related to what we have experienced emotionally with certain colors and feel through them, maybe influenced by early childhood or through other stages of life. When I paint or create an image as an example, how many people see it as I do, see how I created it, the extent of the contrast, the interplay of the color, the charisma of the colors? I strongly suspect that only I see the picture visually as I have created it, which is very sad in one way but very interesting in another way. Unfortunately, I will never be able to see through other eyes and look at my creations in such a way, especially because I believe in how many emotions and feelings are just behind colors and how influential the whole thing can be for a person.

Let's look at the word with a sloping angle and look at it alternately with one eye closed and then with the other eye closed. What happens? See how the word jumps around. How the optical dimension changes. Now if you blink quickly the word will literally dance in front of you. If you approach closer and put your head next to the sheet you can see almost nothing with the lower eye, but with the upper one can still look at it relatively well and with both eyes open it is again completely different.

Every day I play with words and objects in this way, whether in an optical way or solely in my mind. The fascination with which one can look at the world every day is one of my greatest joys in the external as well as in the inner world. The word here is just an example. These games can be played with just about any item, and one can rediscover ubiquitous things every day.

So apart from a lot of little gadgets and things that everyone can find out and change themselves, in the view and playing with just one word we come now to the great, and for me, very impressive finale, of what is possible with a word in a box. We always keep in mind that the box stands for all that we know and represents our consciousness, whether in the external world or within the depths of our consciousness. The lines of the box are what describe our horizon, our box.

We now look at the word until we have it pictorially before us. We close our eyes and look at it from a completely different dimension in our mind; solved from the 2d dimension on the paper and also solved by the 3d dimension we created on the paper. We move away from consideration through our seeing, away from contemplation through the external sense we call seeing. With our eyes closed, we look at the word solely in our consciousness.

What exactly should I call this kind of performance? I can't tell and it doesn't matter what we call it. To be able to see in this way took me many years, many years in which I have reviewed many things, reinvented for myself, many years in which I have gathered very intense rituals and psychedelic experiences. It is neither seen in the sense that we know as seeing and has nothing to do with some kind of two or three-dimensional image. I wish I could reproduce things that I 'see' in this way but this is not even remotely possible for my art or stories stumble and me in a goofy way upon the one percent hurdle of what is happening in my mind.

Now it is important to realize that there are no limits. In our minds, there is no up and no down. No close and no TV. If we just want and allow it, there are no restrictions that limit us in any way.

I love to form patterns and shapes out of that. You can often see them in my art.

I love to create rotating patterns that form each other into something new and have no support in color, shape, and dimension. What I now create out of this in my mind is so absurd, in contrast to anything that I somehow reproduce on a medium outside of my mind in the external world.

Understanding that there are no limits to our imagination is one of the greatest insights and commitments to one's capabilities. And we are still talking solely about the pictorial representation of a word on a piece of paper. However, I am convinced that every person with pure consciousness, who takes the time to look at a single word like this, will see that word differently afterward and that person may then form a new optical association. The person has gone a bit closer to the limit of the perception of his own box, a piece in a direction in which there is no way back into the previous box. Because once you have opened your eyes, it is difficult to close them again. Even though we realize that our previous life was much easier and more comfortable. Even if we wanted to

just take a step back it will not be possible for
us anyway.

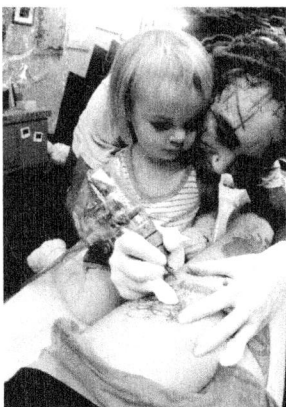

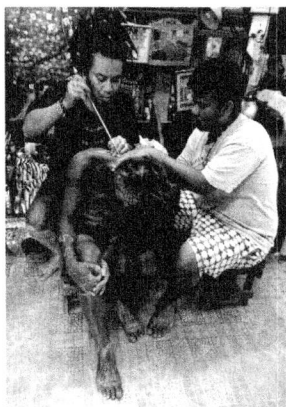

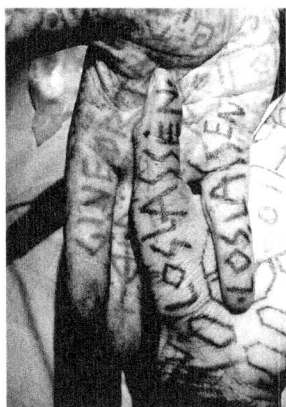

Suppose we live in a world where there is only
water to drink, which is enough to survive and

completely satisfy our needs? Since we don`t know anything else, we have no choice but to drink nothing else but water.

Now suppose one day a situation comes in which we see something ~ let it be a banana shake, something you really like to drink. At this point, you have no idea what it is and how it tastes.

Let's assume someone comes and shows you this drink and tells you that it is the most incredible and tastiest thing you can ever drink. The fatal thing is that you only have this one banana shake and you will never get one again. Now I ask you the question: Will you try it and drink it? And be aware that if you drink something other than water and even if it is only once, the water will taste different afterward. Or rather, that you will then perceive water differently since it is no longer the only drink and you know it. So, you will try something completely new, even if you realize that it will change the rest of your life. I think there are various types of people who approach it differently. I guess I am the kind of person that has already been drinking my shake.

The realization of how much potential freedom you carry within your consciousness was the reason I quit taking any kind of substances or drugs (legal or illegal) 12 years ago as they steal these abilities from me.

Any kind of substance that robs me of this endless possibility in my mind and limits my consciousness has lost any kind of temptation and charm for me. This freedom to go beyond the bounds of his imagination, to daily incorporate this thinking into my life is one of the most important principles I want to integrate.

Wait a minute. We are still in the box. The words were only a small example to describe what I mean by this box. Now let's take a new sheet of paper and paint a new box on it, an empty box.

It symbolizes your box again, your consciousness and knowledge, whether with your external presence, in the form of your body and the knowledge of this external world, or inner in the form of feelings and experiences, even apart from the fact that most of the contents of this box are characterized by external influences that have filled this box. Apart from this, how is this box filled?

It's filled with content in the form of ideas and experiences, within the limit of this box. When we look at this box and understand that even though this box represents all the knowledge and experience that exists in this external world, and even if we carried all the knowledge of this world in us, even then we would still be limited to our own box and its confines. Presumably, our point of view would be stubbornly rooted to the bottom and insoluble in it since this kind of knowledge and the related thought which we have learned has been planted in us by people who have also taken that knowledge from that box. And I'm convinced that the tighter we hold on to learning, the harder it becomes to let go of the assertion that even the entire knowledge of the world is worthless. Let's go beyond the bounds of our box. It's the nothingness, the void, that lets our point of view revolve around within that box as we did earlier with a simple word.

There are many influencing personalities like Einstein, Columbus or Dali, Van Gogh in art, or one of my biggest influences, Evel Knievel. It may be absurd to call these personalities together in one sentence but they were all personalities who realized early on that the limits of what we know are not the limits of reality. All are examples of different people who have broken boundaries and have helped our box to grow a bit, or at least the influence of official history. The partly fundamental elements have been placed in our box because yes, once the world was small and shallow until someday someone sailed over that border and after that nothing was the same until a disc became a ball and nothing was the same as before. Once a border is crossed, the foundation is usually laid for a whole new way, a whole new story, maybe a whole new world.

Let's take an extreme sport of our time. A long time ago Evel Knievel proved that you can jump with a motorcycle. One day someone did a somersault on a motorcycle for the first time in the history of motorcycling but when that limit was crossed, that was the end of the beginning.

Several years later there were already many combinations that athletes did on their motorcycles in addition to a somersault, double somersaults and eventually the first triple somersault. If you had told Evel Knievel 30 years ago that people would be able to do these things on a motorcycle in the future he would have laughed. But once someone has crossed a border, he opens the box for many more. For what man knows makes him less afraid and the step is much easier than sailing into unknown dark waters.

We think that our box is bigger today than it ever was. But actually, it is tiny compared to what could be if we only accept that we are unknowing. For as long as we consider ourselves as knowing, a stone will be a stone and this knowledge will never be doubted. The world is only as big as we know it and nobody will start sailing to prove otherwise. And as long as we believe that it is not possible to do four somersaults on a motorbike, no one will try it.

How far do we even accept this as our box? Is it not the first step to realize this box, push it to its limits of possibilities and, above all, question and dismantle everything, really everything in it? Is it really our own box or do others create it? Is it society or perhaps even by higher powers maybe? What do we know if we only know what is in the box and when the box is filled with the knowledge that is instilled to us by the external world? Does that mean that I should just accept that I am a human being and thus subject to this captivity? Or is even the assumption of what I seem to be, a human being, even a part of this box?

The question is, how far are we aware that we live in a box? Or do we believe that we live freely and this box does not exist? But then is the feeling of free life just another manifestation of what's in this box to give us the feeling of freedom and to make this box as invisible as possible? That is another big topic that I'll talk about later.

Back to the box. Everything is possible. Everything. And everyone who says otherwise says it based on the limits that lie within his box, through the knowledge and thoughts that manifested this attitude in his mind, by influences that were not outside this box. A border is only a limit until it has been breached, and the limits of what is possible are still being postponed because where were our limits in technology and life 50 years ago, 100 years ago, and where are they today?

Is that not proof enough that there are no limits? How far has our box grown and continues to grow every year? And who tells you that you are not the one breaking a line, no matter in what way, creating your own limits or even the limit of what we see in this external world as a box.

Nothing is impossible once you get rid of what was placed in our box. And what is it that is put in the box and what do we carry in us? How well do we know our box and are we able to reach its full potential?

The content of our box

Now let's get to what I like to call the 'manifestation of the basic idea'. First of all, I have to mention that thought is something very absurd and controversial for me. First and foremost, it is my greatest desire to act and live thoughtlessly. I feel the biggest freedom in the moments when I act freely, without considering any thoughts at all. And I do not mean that in spite of other thoughts I decide to listen to my heart or a feeling or inspiration. I mean a complete step back to act out of pure freedom without first processing a thought, whether consciously or unconsciously. But exactly this action in everyday life is almost impossible for me. You simply carry the entire influence of your life in your thoughts with you and every question or action is accompanied by chains of thoughts, mostly in the form of an inner mental balance between right and wrong, legal or illegal, socially accepted or denounced, and so on. Even though my actions are guided by other thoughts nowadays, I still carry with me the kind of thoughts in which I was brought up from infancy, even if I do not pay much attention to them in many moments. Nevertheless, I always carry them with me and they are part of my consciousness.

On one hand, chains of thought are something I strive for, but on the other hand, my entire life consists of and is made up of thought-chains. Nothing that I realized in the external world did not first manifest in my mind. My world in which I try to live is, to a large extent, what I create in my imagination and my thoughts. I will not be able to present or live out what is not possible first in my thoughts. But on the other hand, I guess, it means that it is possible to live out or represent something externally only because it is possible in thought. Only a few things are probably easier to transport from thoughts to reality than others. Personally, I think nothing is impossible.

Back to our thoughts, or should we say 'back to the box'? It's almost the same because the box is mostly made up of our thoughts and our consciousness. So, what are thoughts, emotions, feelings, etc. and where do they come from? How do we know what we know? A tree is a tree. And what we know about it is what we have learned, what was told to us. But how far do we accept that as a perfect reality? How far are we satisfied with what we have been implanted in? Some would say this is a big advantage. Otherwise, we would have to learn everything again like the Stone Age people. But neither would I go as far as to claim that the Stone Age people had a smaller box than we have today, nor would I go so far as to believe that there was such a thing as Stone Age man.

It could be just as historically realistic that man was already much more intelligent and evolved than we are today, and any historical, scientific, archaeological proof and everything that is supposed to give us that belief is just a creation to give us just that feeling and reality.

I realized early on that everything that reflects reality in my head, and in the outer world, is nothing more than the manifestation of the basic idea, what I was given as a child through school and society. These concepts are projected as thoughts from people who live in the same 'template-way' as I should. Any kind of feelings or ideas that I have not made myself from a free experience and a free view, for me, is not my own free knowledge and quite consciously, influenced by external circumstances. Most events in which people begin to 'see' are initiated by other external circumstances, by people wanting to press them into their box, which is nothing more than their template. Therefore, almost no experience is completely free and we are probably caught up for life in absorbing or enduring these external circumstances.

It's a dilemma to which I haven't got an answer or a solution. I'm just as trapped in it as people who are at the same point. I cannot answer "reality" or "human existence" as easily as religion or science can. And I don't think I'll ever get an answer to these questions, or rather, that I'll ever get to know how certain things really are. As I said earlier, everything that I experience in the outside is not necessarily the reality of the truth for me. Maybe this will lose much of its importance when everything meaningful becomes meaningless, you begin to see and appreciate things differently.

It is much easier to accept everything as we have been carrying it for a long time and not to question it. A tree is a tree and on we go.

So when we connect something positive with an object or activity and associate a great feeling with it, then is it really because we have a fulfilling feeling with it? Or is it because of early childhood imprinting that the very thought has been implanted in us to convey that feeling in certain situations?

I believe that one can find bliss and joy in certain things. And I'm more likely to be the one who`s hit negatively by questioning those things and giving up on quick gratification. But a lot that once seemed important and meaningful and gave me the feeling of happiness just does not exist anymore, or rather, in my logic today simply no longer makes sense.

Do we really have a perfect sense of happiness if we have earned a lot of money? Would the pile of money feel so great if we did not have that imprinted idea of it? Would it feel good if one day it was in front of us just like that and we had no idea what it is and would rediscover it? Or does it feel good because we have the association with the feeling that you have with ideas that just feel good about a bunch of money? Did we ever question that and does it not apply to every conceivable feeling or value that we know?

From a normal social perspective, what is a perfectly happy life? Good work. Good means from a normal social point of view, a job where you earn a lot of money and have a beautiful house. Beautiful means, from a normal social point of view, a big, expensive house, and so on. Are such achievements enriching life? Yes, but are such achievements essential to a fulfilling life? Do such achievements live? Do they really bring perfect happiness and a perfect life? Or is it just the association that we have been influenced by from an early age?

Are we striving for such achievements because we strive for it with a perfect heart, and it is the way to bliss, or is it because it is the manifestation of a society that is reflected in our mindset? How far are we free to detach ourselves from the thought or the thought of the feeling behind it?

For most people, it's probably just about feeling good and leaving everything as it is. I do not want to say that one is better than the other. If I went so far then I would rather cherish that the simple life promises much more luck, or that the way to bliss is much easier. A good job and an expensive car are at least goals in mind. My goals, however, are no longer existing and thus in a way never reachable.

Not everyone wants to or has to push boundaries and probably it is for the better if the majority of people live on as usual.

From my point of view, it is not bad to own a house or to do a job in which you make good money. I rather doubt the basic idea that this is the way to fulfillment. In many cases, this basic idea is related to people making decisions against any sense of their heart to lead a life more fulfilling in the view of society or in the view of his own thoughts, which in return only reflects the templates of society. I am probably one of the few who are very radical in their thinking and life.

When we take black and white there are many nuances of gray in between, many fine gradients of what can be in between. They do not exist for me. Things are black or white. Things are real or not real. Everything in between I see as compromises. Either one believes in God or science, not both together as they contradict each other. For either, you believe that a god or gods have created man, or that the theory of evolution is the reason why man exists on earth. I do not deny all this. Everything can be possible. Nevertheless, I believe in what I already know or heard. For me, any human theory is nothing more than a shade of gray.

I think it is easier to lead a fulfilled life from the point of view of a normal and socialized person rather than from my point of view with the good thought in the background as I lost all sense for what a fulfilling life could be. On the other hand, my life fulfills itself just by living, simply living. Even though through this setting there is never such a thing as a complete goal that I can or want to achieve. Every new day is as it is~ New.

Ironically, I don't have a perfect goal that I work towards. It is more that I work towards living. When living it is not accepted, even that becomes a big step. But it seems so easy to live.

With the fact of doubting and questioning everything, to what extent is it possible to break away from your basic thoughts and build completely new frames of mind and structures?

The attempt to realize this is already the first small step. And again, the question arises, if one wants to take this step at all. Are you willing to question everything and the depth of yourself, possibly giving up a very simple happy life for a path without a goal?

Once you open your eyes there is usually no turning back. The moment you move and bend the boundaries of your box, shift the view in your box, you understand that no matter what perspective you look at this box from, nothing reflects your own reality perfectly.

Then and only then, you will probably find it almost impossible to find something like bliss within this box. Because any kind of bliss that is felt within this box, and the origins and guidelines associated with it, is just a pre-implanted sense of it, a feeling to guide us and lead us to certain actions, to control us, so to speak. Because if we all did not work the way we should, it would not work that way. Then there would be no society and no being together. Because your freedom ends where the freedom of your neighbor begins. And just as the world as we know it is populated and occupied, just as the human form of existence behaves, a perfect free way of life would never work. Probably the human was never intended and if so, then the Stone Age man still had the freest form of life in my eyes.

Yes, control is a hard word. But let's face it; none of us are completely free in this outer world.

Fear.

Probably it is the biggest weapon of society. Or

more clearly, the greatest weapon of any belief system, religion, or institution that guides and controls people. But how deep is this fear really real in us, or is it just another implanted sense of society?

Why do we have any fears at all? For example, the fear of losing one's job keeps so many people from quitting a job in which they are unhappy and not satisfied. Rather, they are clinging to it, hoping that one day something better will be put at their feet. The fear is satisfied with it and thus, in a very absurd way, also their own satisfaction. Or is it alternately an acceptance of the situation that offers this kind of satisfaction? Fear has so many facets to control people, but more on that later.

Now let's go back to our box. Consider the idea of accepting that our thoughts have been influenced and are always guided. Now we put an imaginary word in our box, which in turn reflects a thought. Take, for example, the word and the feeling of fear; that fear of not having an apartment and thus being homeless. And I suspect that we almost all carry this fear somewhere in us. The question that arises is just, "why"?

Have we ever been homeless? Have we ever lived outside and stayed without having a real solid place we call our home. Do we really have this experience ourselves and therefore is it a reasonable fear of being homeless?

How would it be if we decide by our free will to be homeless? What if we decide to give up our apartment and with it all obligations and live outside for a year, or in a car, or just move around and find a new sleeping place every day?

Yes, then we would really be putting ourselves in a situation to find out.

Up to now is it the experience that has shaped us or it is the manifestation of the fear that has been planted in us that ultimately guides us? Are we more than joyfully and blindly jumping into the situation and defying it, experiencing and absorbing it to allow ourselves to finally draw our own experience?

To take that feeling and, as before, the word in the box completely rediscovered, to comprehend the origin of it and to build up its new association, your own association, based on what I call free knowledge.

And yes, maybe it means throwing away this job and becoming homeless. Perhaps this can be a much greater fulfillment and an adventure than what your life has ever given to you. But as long as you are controlled by fear you will never find out, and you may wonder what your life would have been.

Society is more aware of this than most and if everyone went off to discover life we'd have a big problem here. The world as we know it would not work anymore and I do not believe that there will ever be a social life form that will give all living creatures a real free choice over their lives.

How far are we capable and willing to detach now not only from the optical intuition of this word but also from its meaning? And with meaning I mean the manifestation of the meaning that lies within our heads, the meaning and feelings and events we associate with this or that word. How free and uninhibited can we now look at this word and consider this feeling without being burdened?

What is fear? Where does it come from?

These are questions that I ask myself again and again. But fear is just another example of a feeling that we wrote in our box before. Especially in consciousness-expanding states of any kind, such games are more than interesting, as in to find out why one associates and feels certain feelings and sensations as one does.

The perfect objective consideration is still far away in the long run to permanently change such deep-drawn trains of thought and mindsets. To which extent it is even possible to consciously change such deep trains of thought is questionable. It is more likely that through multiple realizations of certain feelings and thoughts my consciousness merely adjusts these newly gained associations and conveniently updates itself. So, it may be more of an awareness that leads to a change in consciousness rather than a purposeful controlled change of consciousness.

Those little moments, when I am deep in my consciousness when I have moments of realization, are the few moments when I feel and call perfect freedom. This may be something that many people say who have combined psychedelic substances and experienced such or similar moments. Regardless, I have many "perfect freedom" moments through other rituals and definitely even at sexual climaxes.

In this state, the perfect objective consideration, no external influences or impressions occupy my worldview but I freely experience what I see or feel.

Again, it can be argued how free it really is because, in a way, I am dependent on certain situations, rituals, events or substances and even so, I have no complete control of what happens and where it takes me. Also, I can never tell if this situation brings me to a moment of freedom.

And, even if it were specifically possible for me to control this situation, there is always the starting point as a human being within my preloaded and pre-implanted box.

I just say to myself that it is possible to feel and receive absolute freedom in such moments and over the years I have learned from experience how I can easily get myself into such moments. But I'll never get perfect control of it, and even if it strives to exist in such a state, it's likely to be denied to me as a human being.

Also, it is probably wishful thinking that I can close my eyes and direct such a condition in a controlled manner. Maybe you can view the whole thing as a dilemma and say that it is then never possible to feel complete freedom.

But I see these few moments rather as enrichment and would like to miss them in no case, even though I am aware that I have to give up a constant sense of freedom. But since I do not particularly believe in the possibility of permanent perfect freedom since this is anyway only an already pre-implanted idea, I don't really give up anything but I just accept things in the range of my possibilities.

Take a big jar and pour a can of Coke into it. The cola should now reflect our worldly ideas. Any new experience now that is outside of our box and our mindset, we now add water in the form of a teaspoon. One or two teaspoons are not too much and you would hardly notice them in the Coke. But over time, as more and more teaspoons of water are added, our basic substance eventually changes radically. It changed from a watery coke to a drink, which is then significantly more water than coke until the day arrives that you cannot taste the coke anymore.

Nevertheless, we are aware that this coke is still available and can never be filtered out of the drink. This is how similar I see it with our thoughts and the freedom of how we can direct and direct ourselves more. Maybe even our preprogrammed ideas can mix down as far as not to taste much of it, in which we go to ourselves in many moments where we objectively gather new experiences so far to shake them up piece by piece with our previous ones.

But no matter how much we experience and how much free knowledge we absorb and whatever we experience, our pre-implanted basic ideas in the form of cola will never get out of the depths of our consciousness and much less out of our subconscious.

I already mentioned that the thoughts are very absurd and ambiguous for me. Since on one hand, they keep me away from freedom but on the other hand, I can be completely thought-free in the depths of my consciousness, again mostly based on thoughts.

Or built up by pictures, feelings, impressions, and experiences, which in return were somehow processed in, thought inwardly. Maybe the word thought is not the right word to convey what I mean. Let's call it my inner voice, my inner me, in a way, my consciousness.

But yes, when my thoughts represent my consciousness and I define myself as my consciousness then, for the most part, I am influenced by the external

44

environment, which in turn has shaped much of my consciousness.

Take the word "thought" and put it in our box. What are thoughts?

We have them daily in our consciousness, or for me and as I define them, they are our consciousness. They may be more ourselves than how we enter the outer world through our human shell. We all think and experience things in our thoughts that we do not share with others and that we do not externally live out.

I am a relatively open and honest person and have little shame and inhibitions. Nevertheless, I experience myself often enough to experience things in my thoughts that I would never live out or share with anyone, maybe even thoughts that scare you and you'd wonder where they come from.

Your own freedom ends where the freedom of another begins. But true freedom would have no end and would be infinite. Your own interpretation of your thoughts ends where the expression of your fellow human's thoughts begins.

But in how far are our thoughts really our own thoughts and not pre-marked good of thought? Which in return is just to let us live and think just as we should in the eye of societal life and thought. Life and thinking, as we want it to be, is something we probably have not even learned.

And even if we want to live life as we do and think about how we want to think, then we are still free from the thoughts of how we should actually live and function.

How often do we have small mind battles, entanglements, and little men in your head telling you what to do, etc?

Would it not be the greatest freedom to do just that and become completely free in your own mindset? Would we then have spontaneous machines that would only act without knowing what they are doing? I was told that it takes exactly this balance to character strength, authenticity and for a personality to form. Yes, exactly these considerations that let you know where you stand.

Personally, I think it's a pity that it probably needs this and you are mostly defined and developed by others. Yes, there is positive and negative. If I gave it all up, I would probably be more of a Stone Age person again without much knowledge in the sense that we define as knowledge. But I would be less myself or more myself. I can only puzzle and speculate about that. I even use the knowledge and the technology that today's life offers us and do not want to miss it to express my art and myself, as it is possible nowadays. However, I would not go so far as to say that living without all this is worse and less rewarding.

Some steps are also difficult in reverse. But maybe everything is more connected than we like and we should always have the belief that we are so much better off than the generations before us. We may have more possibilities in one way or another, but we have far less to live on than perhaps the generations before us. Because a lot of what we consider to be fundamentally important did not exist in the past and so you had to worry less about it. You were probably more yourself than you might be today.

To be thoughtless

That is probably my greatest aspiration and the possibilities that would be connected would be, in my eyes, infinite, probably not as infinitely as if we carry these considerations in us, but more unbiased and free. Once you've broken all boundaries and fears and everything that has guided you that far, what would you be capable of as a human being in the outer world as well as in the inner depth of your consciousness? You would then have no comparison and could not say that it is more, but it would feel like more. It would feel freer.

How far our manipulated ideas differ from our newly learned, free ideas, we have already noted. Can we even speak of ideas here or would it make sense to manifest this newly learned, newly experienced mindset in something other than in thought? I call it free knowledge, but this too is just a word and again does not express what it represents for me. For even this word 'thought' or the word 'knowledge' is for me already too negatively burdened and shaped to put this new, beautiful enrichment into words. In my imagination, the best thing to do would be to completely let go of what I call manipulated thought and actions, and to solely rely on free knowledge as our own new thought, our free knowledge is the water we pour into the coke.

Now, if we say that our life is based more on free knowledge rather than clinging to the old pre-implanted knowledge, how far will it influence and guide us and possibly enable us to live as we have always wished?

For if we once based our decisions on free knowledge rather than on existing thought, then our actions will also be freer and more informal, maybe even significantly less or one day perhaps even almost no longer steered by foreign influences and the associated manipulation no matter when and how this manipulation took place. The process of balancing between the already existing thoughts and the newer free knowledge will probably never fade out the little men who want to tell me how to live, still at war with the thoughts that just will not let me act as I just think it's right, right in the sense of how it feels right when I turn off my thoughts.

Only the complete realization of this and the related separation between these two processes have led me to look at many things and situations differently and make decisions from a different angle.

And the more water is in our glass in the long run, the easier it will be to add more. Because every new decision and experience is much easier to do once we learn how to enrich it.

Until maybe one day we may be pure enough to not notice much of the coke anymore and drink the water safely. And by drinking I mean to live, to truly live without the influence of society and its pre-implanted thoughts, and everything related to it.

Specially well-read or studied people, or in the eye of society, intelligent people, in my eyes have it much harder to solve this. What does it mean to be intelligent, wise or intellectual? Or rather, from what point of view are any of these kinds of already manipulated ideas keeping people more inside of their boxes? Knowledge is power. Is that really so, and even if it were, power would bring us freedom, or would it just bind us more?

I also think that out of sheer laziness or complete refusal, one should not decide to take any knowledge. Knowledge is exciting and interesting and definitely helps you understand more about how things might or may not be. Unfortunately, many people cling to their already existing knowledge and see it as truth.

From this point of view, I would say that it is much easier for people who are more ignorant to take in free knowledge than people who consider themselves to be wise. These, in turn, will only cling to what we call knowledge and a completely new perspective is no longer so easy to accept. Let's call them the coca cola-people. If knowledge is nothing more than the controlled information that society allows us to absorb, a society that pours us coke as if there was nothing else to drink.

Somehow I find the entire knowledge of this world to be useless when it comes to creating your own view of the world. Knowing everything that can be taken up by books, media, teachers, etc., is biased in some way and may only be part of keeping us in a template. Rather, it is all about theories. Whether and how far there is evidence for anything is to doubt anyway. There is a variety of starting points and views. But a believer has just as much evidence for a god as a scientist has for the theory of evolution. If, for example, you doubt the Earth itself, you do not believe in gravity. If you doubt man in himself, you also do not believe in evolution.

Once you doubt the whole knowledge of the world, it

also means that it no longer represents knowledge as we believe to know. This does not mean that there can be nothing meaningful or interesting anymore.

But you definitely do not give the whole belief and meaning any more credit than it should have. Everything is possible and realistic in a way. But equally, everything is meaningless and unrealistic in a different way.

It is probably in each self how much attention he or she gives to any form of knowledge and how he lets his life, thinking and acting lead from it.

The limitation of our box

Now we come to the next step or the next consideration.

Now that we are aware of what our box is, how it is filled, and where its boundaries are, let's take our piece of paper and review this box again.

Consider the idea that we are as free as possible to travel around inside this box and create freely, actually able to manifest a viewpoint within the box, now free to move and place yourself anywhere within this box. What if you can move anywhere in the box in every dimension?

Just as we have tried to look at a word or a feeling inside this box, is it possible for us to view and analyze our entire box as well? Call it self-analysis, the solution of its ego, its ego, the objective consideration of its self. No matter what we call it or how we call it. For me, it's always a big overcoming for something new, a big hurdle to let go of you and to confront yourself.

What we are going to do is this:

We paint a new box around our existing box and we paint our point of view down into the box. Since the moment this box is aware of us and we create a new reality with it, we also create a new box. A box in which we are aware of the box in which we live.

Our new point of view below is the point of view from my current moment view and from the experiences you have just read, a point of view with the idea of a thought, which does not have to correspond to your own. Because all you have read is nothing more than my train of thought, which in turn are just as influenced and influenced by foreign ideas.

To understand that my box is not nearly what reflects in your box is an important step.

And now, again, we are trying to solve this view, which is my or your view. Now that we are aware that any kind of viewpoint is entirely influenced and manipulated, even if you create a view for yourself and then completely hold on to it, you will prevent yourself from moving on. Then you will also just create a new box that keeps you from discovering new things and question things.

Until which point is it possible for us to free ourselves from our ego, to detach ourselves from ourselves and to really look at our box completely free and objectively? Meaning the box that represents our consciousness and our person. How far can we circle around it and look at it from all sides and question our box in every way? If there is no dimension, no color, no boundaries, and no horizon or manipulated view anymore. So then to which degree are we satisfied with what we call our box?

Any fundamental accomplishments, qualities, and goals that we carry within us are really what will make us completely happy. Is it really the things that we seek that will guide us to perfect bliss, or are they manifestations that we carry within us of things that are only meant to convey bliss? Bliss is a manifestation of a perfect life but achieved from what point of view and at what price?

If we assume that our thoughts and the feelings behind them are influenced by how society wants us to live, how far do we live according to our own intuition? After our hearts and our dreams?

Maybe I repeat myself. But not all of us live in a kind of repetition. Years of my life I wasted with a day-to-day life to live out in a repeat. Get up every day at the same time to do the same work.

Apart from the fact that I could never really fit in or adapt, I really did try. But I never really got used to it either at school or in a social or family level. I was a kid that always made trouble, or was I just a kid that somehow did not fit into the whole thing? And what happens if you do not adapt and insert enough as a child? You will be punished and you will be taught that you are bad. The question is not whether to adept the school to the child, but rather that the child has to be adapted to the school.

When I think about my past, it makes a lot of sense. And I do not want to whine about my childhood or my past. But when I think about it now, I realize that I was probably never destined to fit into normal life.

How do Authorities react to such a child? They

respond with even more pressure and punishment to push someone into the mask.

Let's take a quick look at my past. As an unwanted child, I witnessed the divorce of my parents while still very young. This involved a hate dispute between my parents and the custody dispute over the visitation rights of my father. Soon after I lost all contact with my father. Through the manipulative influence of my mother, I believed him to be a very negative character and held bad feelings for him, which turned out to be very wrong. This negativity did not help much with my early childhood character development and molding.

My mother kicked me out of the house shortly after my fifteenth birthday whereupon I moved in with my divorced and single-living grandmother, a very conservative woman with all sorts of old fashioned concepts. My right to live at her place was subject to many conditions, so I started job training against my will. I only longed for it throughout my school years in order to leave them behind me. But that would have been my final step to street life at that time. What can I say? I was a kid and didn't know any better. The older I got, the more I realized that the normal social way has become indisputable to me and the confrontations at home escalated more and more, especially when I started to change my body in a very visible way relatively early to give me more power on my own way.

The actual story I wanted to tell is the following: At some point, relatively early, I had thrown all my school records and important papers and documents into the trash bin. My grandmother fished all my papers out of the trash bin and kept them hidden for me, for a time in which I will come to my senses after her statement, "and then you will be grateful for it."

Unfortunately, this was denied for her and so she gave me all my documents a few years ago. Whether it was really just for the reason that I have a few memories of my youth or whether it was a last attempt to 'wake up' I cannot say exactly. But I have my guess.

With an entire life in between and a neutral, objective assessment of it, I let much of it through me. And I do not just mean grades. I mean, letting go as I was judged and felt scrutinized by authoritarians at that early age.

It started already at the age of 6 years that I seemed to be a child who just could not or did not want to integrate. And so it reads through all the testimonies until I had finished school at some point. If it had been up to me I would have left it behind sooner. But that was not in my power at the time. Or rather, I simply was not aware of my power over my life.

I ask myself in retrospect why nobody acts in cases like these. And I mean acting for a child, to be adult in a place or in a situation where a child cannot feel well and prosper. Why not help instead of allowing the child to believe that he or she is wrong forcing them to only try harder to adapt?

Obviously, there must have been reasons to resist something over such a long distance. But most parents just want their child to have a 'good' life later on. And a good life does not mean a happy life, at least not if the idea of happiness is different than your own and unfortunately I had to experience this for myself. Many people around me had to experience it also. Most likely, not every person is an adaptation machine.

Later on, I burned everything that would be important to most people. This time there was no more solicitation to free me or prevent me from taking a step backward. This time, I made it purely out of the feeling that all this was really and completely insignificant for me.

I had already let go of it and it was nice to see it again in a different way and different than my grandmother wanted. I was very grateful that she gave me this moment, to experience once again how important and right this step was in my life. I probably would not have my life without this step.

And I really tried. I wanted to be `normal`.

Actually, I so very much wanted to do something artistic. Throughout my childhood and school days, I was painting and creating. I was told that I had an eye and a talent for art. But how was my promotion of these qualities in the end? At school, I had art classes 45 minutes a week.

Yet we had 135 minutes of religious instruction. Even though I did not have any faith in Christianity at this time. Those 45 minutes of artistic promotion in the only thing that has really given me something and with which I now define my entire life. What would I have been able to do if I had been promoted and supported as a child instead of trying without reward to adapt myself?

This I'll never know.

At that time I would have had to go to school for a career in most of the artistic professions and in some cases would even have to study. But that was just not possible. I was so happy to finish the school chapter that it did not cost me much of a thought to decide.

I wanted to work a bit to be able to focus more on my art as the last years of my life I'd had to sacrifice the majority of my time for school.

Another condition for me to stay at my grandmother's was that I start an education to learn something 'reasonable'. And so I started training as a gardener. At that time, it was near my place of residence and it was reasonably well paid. Since I was somehow aware that I never work in this profession, it was not that significant anyway.

It was another thing I was socially forced to do and perhaps even important to fully realize that I have to break away from it to somehow find fulfillment in my life.

It was more than time to start living.

I do not blame anyone either. Because even teachers, parents and other authoritarian persons have not learned otherwise and are firmly convinced that this is the right way. But at some point, you will turn your back on your family, friends and many other people who once seemed important to you. At some point, that just does not make Sin any more.

At some point, it's time to let go and stop dreaming of a life.

What are dreams?

Once you have realized that any kind of what we call a "dream" is just an idea that is inside this box. Since everything we know, think and feel, even knowledge material, is what is already inside this box, built from ideas and suggestions from this box known to us.

Once we realize that every dream or wish is inside this box, nothing is impossible. The moment you say to yourself that a dream can never be realized that is the moment you create something like a smaller box outside this box.

To understand that there is no outside to this box, in the form of knowledge that we already have in us, makes us look at things again.

To understand that nothing is impossible with the right focus, let's approach things differently.

The moment you let go of everything that prevents you from realizing your dream, you will realize this core idea, this dream, more consciously and differently.

This dream becomes a vision and a vision is something tangible. Something realistic. Something for which it is worth giving up other things and aiming for this vision purposefully.

And once one has created one's own reality, no one else will ever be able to influence us and impose on us a reality in which this dream, or later that vision, is unattainable.

Everyone has the choice, but I'll get to that later.

The box with all its limitations:

What does that mean? How far have we already created and perceived our own reality to accept that the boundaries we know are the boundaries that make up our own reality?

My biggest passion for everything I do in life is probably finding my limits and taking one step beyond. The feeling it conveys is indescribable.

I mean the feeling of freedom, the feeling of having no access to already manipulated ideas, to have no trains of thought and the associated thoughts jumble that comes with them.

These are moments of freedom because such an experience is something that is not inside your box. That is, everything that you absorb and experience with this new experience is created solely from 100 percent free pure thought.

This is what I call the so-called free knowledge.

Free knowledge.

Let's take Body suspension for example:

Suspensions are one of many old shamanic rituals that I have gone through a lot in my life and go through again and. It is something that has greatly enriched my life. But what exactly is a suspension ritual?

It means that your skin is pierced with special hooks and then you get pulled up until you finally hang freely in the air. Pain is part of the whole but not the significant part. It is rather that one has to accept the pain for this experience. In general, we are like animals and other living beings, living and feeling beings genetically programmed to avoid pain. Or rather, it is our instinct to survive that which guides us first to ward off anything that could harm us. And so it does not make any sense to do something silly to pierce hooks through your skin, to hang in the air.

But what is behind it? What is the similarity or what has this to do with our box?

Simple. What does the idea, that a person hangs on hooks trigger in us? And I do not mean to ward off our natural instincts for harm and pain. Because we do not have to fear anyone when something like this happens to us if we do not decide it for ourselves.

I mean, what does it trigger in many who have never seen such a thing? And over the years, I have experienced a lot of reactions in such moments.

Disgust. Above all, disgust is pretty much the first reaction of many. Followed by the idea of inhuman pain and mental disorder.

But where do these thoughts and feelings come from, when you have never experienced it yourself or when you were in such a ritual? How can a simple picture or narrative trigger such a feeling? How can we pretend to judge something we do not know? And I do not mean the judgment of the people doing this; I mean the judgment of their own feelings. Why are we so predisposed that we are not completely neutral when something new comes up? Where does it come from?

Exactly! Out from our box.

This non-neutrality was planted in us as well. Everything new and unfamiliar generates negativity at first, especially if there are things normally unseen within our society, things that the system is afraid of, things that inspire people to think and question. Yes, then the good old 'morality' comes into play. What is right and what is wrong? We are told, deeply rooted in our consciousness, that this is not good. This is something immoral and bad in the eye of society, even sick perhaps.

Well, fear is always part of how we are held and guided. Now how far are we capable or better, even willing to really let go of such a thing?

Let's take something like a 'normal' body suspension with the hooks in the back. Something that physically every human being can do.

And because body-suspension rituals have been practiced around the world for centuries and are even mimicked by millions in our modern culture, we know that it is physically possible for every human and that it can be made externally as a simple ritual that is within the framework of our worldly box. For many of us, however, it is not yet in our box.

Now let's take a body suspension that we now know that we are physically capable of doing such a ritual.

How far is it possible for us now to go so far in our minds and fully accept that such an experience is something beyond our imagination, something that is not yet in the content of our box, but still worldly possible.

How far can we let go and accept this experi-ence?

And now I go so far and just say cheekily, "there's only one way to find out". There is only one way to go beyond this limit and realize with the help of this experience that there is no such thing as real borders. You have to go to the limit to find out.

Because as long as you sit at home and say to yourself that you are not capable of something. As long as you continue to be guided by pre-implanted thoughts and as long as you do not have your own experience to let go to the limits of your head you will never know if you can take this step. How should one know if one couldn't sail beyond the end of the world if one avoids the fear of sailing off at all?

Once a person has undergone such a ritual and found that he must approach a cause only with the right, open attitude, then there will be no limits and such a ritual will have a lasting effect on their entire life.

When one discovers what is possible, no matter in outward form or manipulated form over their own thoughts, then one will find a great enrichment in new things.

And then, if you really go to the very edge of your limits, you will most likely go the very last step. Because that is then the smallest and most beautiful step on this path.

"Let go!" it says.

Once you drop your fears and you're standing in the middle of the forest with some freaks, already having hooks in your back, knotted on a pulley and standing on tiptoes and basically hanging, then you will know!

Once you've reached that limit; the limit of what you think is feasible and what is in your box. Then you will lift your feet with a smile and jump with a raised feeling of happiness beyond these limits. Because this last step of all steps is actually no longer a step. In most rituals, the essentials happen much earlier than in the rituals themselves. Much has already gone on in your mind mentally and you are already so far along that you are ready for it, otherwise you would not be capable of certain rituals involved. In many tribes, religions, and cultures there were and are various forms of preparation, no matter if the rituals are physical or psychedelic ceremonies. Often one fasts or makes other preparations that interrupt the normal daily routine so as to remember over and over again and thereby become mentally prepared.

I myself have participated in rituals in Asia where people prepare for an entire year. Over such a long period this preparation builds upon itself and when it finally comes to the end, the human is literally bursting from what has accumulated emotionally, mentally and hormonally. And I can say it's so beautiful to witness something like that. Even in a foreign country and with people you cannot even communicate a word with. But the whole thing does not need any big words and many of the rituals that I experienced were relatively free from human words.

If you cling too much to your fears, you'll never even come close to getting into such a situation and you'll never experience what it means to override a limit and with it your own imagination.

Your box will change. It will enlarge and your boundaries will shift. And next time you will do such a body suspension and it will feel more normal.

You will not have that ignorant feeling anymore, the fear you had when that thing was still something unknown and inexperienced. Now you have created your own association within your own box.

But the feeling that you once had, when you crossed the border blind, will never be achieved again when you repeat the same experience because it has already manifested itself in you and no longer represents a limit.

To name but one of many external rituals that we are very easily able to leap beyond the limit of our thinking, the body suspension is just one example of a very nice ritual in my eyes.

For who tells us what is in the range of what we can do, or who defines the realm of the possible in the first place?

Especially when you have experienced such a ritual for the first time in your life, when you have consciously crossed a boundary of your own existence for the first time, and then a lot will change within you.

Even today, I refer to the body suspension as one of the most extreme forms of human modification, even if only a few small scars remain on the outside. The inner change through such a ritual, which is denied in the right circumstances and the right motivation, is far stronger than anything else you can change with his external shell as a human being.

By that, I do not mean just the specific ritual or the respective act of it. I am solely speaking from the experience of going to the ultimate of its limit and taking one step beyond. And just the experience gained from it that allows us to understand that any border you carry in itself, is just an illusion and nothing more than a huge wall, a huge obstacle that prevents one from living.

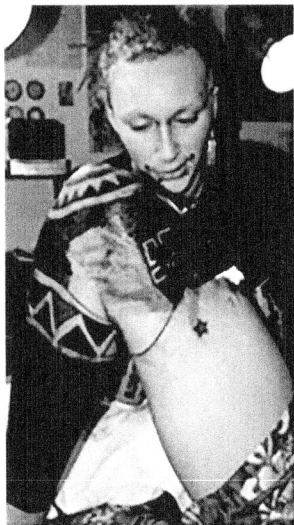

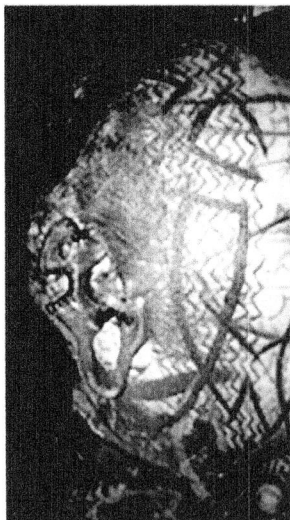

Passing this border leads you to understand that nobody or nothing can tell you what is possible or not. If you understand what you think is impossible, it just was not part of your imagination and not a part of your own box yet.

But maybe our box is just waiting for a fresh update and the past proves more than anything else how the limits of our imagination have wandered. What we call life today and what it means was not nearly conceivable many years ago.

If you tried 40 years ago to explain the internet to someone, telling them that at some point we would all be running around with handheld devices that allow anyone to access almost everything in the world they'd all have thought you mad and laughed at you. Consider how technology has developed over the last generations. Once it was incredible that you could call someone located on another continent. It was even once unbelievable that there are even other continents.

But from a former 'wow' of such news, we have concluded that it has become a perfectly normal part of our lives, a step further away from what we call stone age man to be so connected.

This is the 245.874.689 update of the former Stone Age man. So, assuming, of course, that you even believe in something like the theory of evolution, in which there was something like an underdeveloped person at all. But an update can be effective. Definitely, small errors in the system are ironed out.

The big box of the world is updated almost daily.

Well, "Box Basic", so to speak.

Now let's pick up our sheet of paper with our already drawn box again.

Now let's go this far and just put our viewpoint outside this box. Meanwhile, our own worldview has shifted and this has changed the picture of our box.

Any kind of borderline experience can trigger something like that. It is well known that any kind of crossing of borders that burns deep into our thoughts is so developmental in its way that it also changes our lives sustainably.

The first step is to move on in each case mentally. To come so far in our consciousness as to even create the basis for an external life change.

And that may sound like a fit-for-fun weight loss program for fat people, but an external change is most likely always guided by something internal. Otherwise, it is doomed to failure and you will experience little fulfillment with the outer change.

Think outside the box.

Live outside the box.

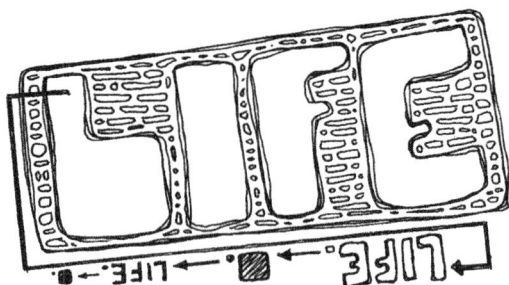

Old familiar sentences:

Are we aware of how far these two sentences are in harmony with each other? One thing does not work without the other. Both are part of the whole and might be part of the same realization. You could also say that one thing leads to another, no matter in which order you experience or experience it.

Maybe it is a purely external experience that opens you the inner limit so far and thus influences your life afterward.

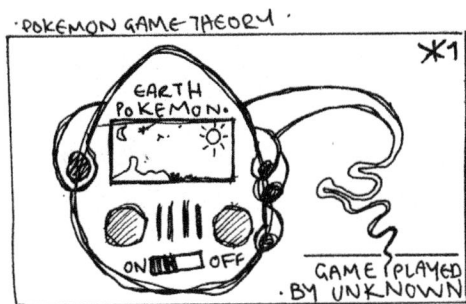

Perhaps it is a purely an inward experience, only in your thoughts that touch you so much as to change your reality in the long term.

Often there are many of these steps, back and forth, which let you slowly out of the box. Let them walk at least slowly and curiously to the edge of this box. Once on the edge, the last step in my eyes is the easiest as then the focus and the will be already strong enough to lead you there, to let one go that far.

And if you can already see over the edge and it is only a small step into a new world, then nothing can stop you.

And with Box, I always mean your own box; your own consciousness, whereby your consciousness is also part of the consciousness of the society in which you have been socialized.

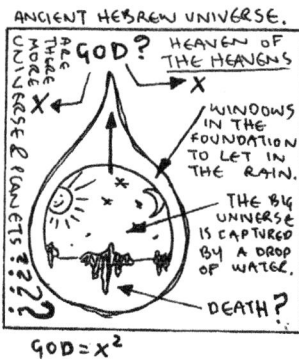

And yes, now we look at our box and our point of view, outside this box and see how free we are with this new view, how free we are to create a new world view for ourselves.

Long ago I became aware that even the recognition of this box and the transgression of my own box is nothing more than the creation of a new worldview, even if this creation, in turn, has brought me to the external cognition and way of life that I've led since then.

However, one does not create anything else but a new view of one's own box, which in turn manifests itself in such a way that one considers it in turn as reality or truth, almost an update of your own box, a new creation of his box but not more important than the previous box.

Where do I set my point now? Where is my view and way of thinking now?

I set it right here, below the box. And to add even more on top, we now draw a new box around our old box, because our box is nothing but a new box. And our view is nothing more than an idea of what we have as a view of the new box. Our box has grown and grown, above all, from free and unprejudiced ideas, from experiences and experiences, maybe from the said free knowledge, maybe even with the pure feeling of freedom that was associated with it.

But our new box is still pretty small, filled with too much of this thought that is already biased and manipulated. Thoughts that are so deeply rooted in our consciousness and subconscious that it is impossible for us to completely erase them.

From my point of view, it is still not bad that we have created a new box.

On the contrary, every new box is great and brings a new, a limit that you can explore and cross. The whole game starts again.

I would describe the whole as a cycle of 'life', much like the Tibetans' life and death in 'The Wheel of Life'. So this whole thing occurs to me because you somehow die with the crossing of each border and then are reborn in a way with the re-creation of the new box.

The nice thing about it is that you live a part of free in his new box, or better formulated, in the life that the new box brings with it. And you also take over his consciousness from the last life, just as the Tibetans do it at rebirth. As a result, the old, where you have already learned from his mistakes and do not make them again, already shape the new life.

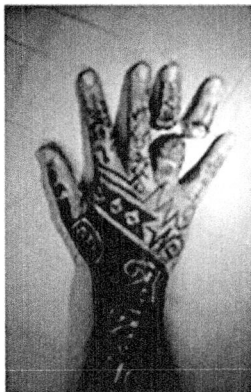

Thus, directly with an update by launches, we arrive at

Human 2.0 = Box 2.0 = live 2.0.

And so the cycle goes on and on and on...

But how free can you be as a human being at all or become aware of the fact that you are constantly living in a box? Does one have anything to do with the other?

Is one free when living in a cage whose existence you do not know, or is one freer when one is aware of the cage and exploits it to the last corner until one day some small loopholes are found?

One could say that the feeling of freedom is purely dependent on mental status. Both can bring freedom in many different ways, though we would still live in a cage physically.

Can you just say, that you are only free once you feel not free or disburdened in English? Or is external freedom not bound to the feeling of freedom? As an example:

I do not feel like a human being. Am I a human or not?

Outwardly of my appearance and my existence, I am definitely what we call human. And although I do not feel that way, I still cannot deny that I am human.

What I want out of is that you can feel free, even though you are aware of captivity.

Whereby freedom in my eyes is always a purely inward feeling because we as human beings will never be free.

The complete acceptance of this box, and with it the complete acceptance of our social imprisonment, does not, from my point of view, have much effect on the inner freedom we can obtain. Our inner freedom does not depend so much on external circumstances.

But this insight, in turn, has a big impact on the way we decide to live inside this box and how big we can be our boxes in the future.

The strongest and purest feelings and emotions are for me each with the most negative together and are therefore a very brutal nature.

How strong does one become aware of the freedom when one lives in captivity? You cannot think about anything else, and your whole life is all about freedom.

Like love and hate. The more you love something with all your heart, the more you want to protect it and the more you are afraid to lose it. And I'm going so far as to say that you even start to hate other things and they're going to be thoroughly annoying. The one you love the most, you hate in the moments where you hurt or wrest this love.

Without love, there would be no hatred. There is no freedom without captivity.

It would be obsolete and one would not work without the other, at least not with the intensity, as we know it.

It just might not be so appreciated, at least not to an intensity as you might feel if you have the complete opposite and know, no matter in which direction.

This topic leads us now to the next point; one of my words in what I call 'my box'.

LIFE 2.0

Reality

When I use the word 'life', I do not mean life in the form of the human existence system, but I mean the way in which we consciously live. The art and the way that we understand the world is a better picture of this illusion whereby we are back in the manifestation of our basic ideas. But how far do we keep in mind that these thoughts represent our reality? How can we influence and guide our reality? How are we, in our consciousness, creating our own lives? What actually tells us what reality is or what life is? And who tells us what life is not?

The answer is: no one else but ourselves, if we let it happen. But how do we reach this point of realization? How is it possible for us considering everything we have learned?

In my younger years I read a lot. How do we consider philosophical works, religions, worldviews, and what about crazy conspiracy theories up to the very logical sounding scientifically "proven" facts? From this I had put together a variety of ideas. And yes, in my eyes, everything is possible and I refuse none of it. Whether the world and man appeared spontaneously, whether the science is correct about the theory of evolution, whether everything we know is just a microcosm or an atom of something else, everything can be possible and I am in no way solidified to any one thing or concept.

If we compare man with all the living forms of life, is that the difference between humans that drives dolphins, monkeys, or something else from intelligent life to earth? How far do we really believe that man is earthly? There were quite a few theories and stunts in my previous life. But how meaningful are they really? How much do they enrich or change your life?

After a few years, I have come to realize that all the information that exists is associated with a great enrichment that's already preloaded. Other than that, it does not affect my life and my reality. But on the contrary, the more you cling to something, the more you believe in something, then the harder it is to let go of it. The harder it is, the more impossible it becomes to build up our own reality and live in it because we live just as we should live and read everything we want to read. There is something suitable for everyone. If you just search long and far enough, you can find the right answer. Because there is probably no theory that has not lived through some time and of course with all sorts of words, data, facts and blablabla...

But actually, none of that matters anymore when you doubt everything.

What does it ascertain, if something is scientifically proven, if you sometimes question that our entire social system is built to let us live in an idyllic delusion? Somehow everything is controlled and what used to be religion has been modernized today by science or some other more up-to-date means.

But how far does that all correspond to reality? Earlier, when there was no science, it was religion that gave people answers. Explanations of life, existence and death and what may follow after that were all provided by religious doctrines or principles. But for thousands of years, more and more people have doubted what was once accepted as reality and created a new one.

Similarly, we are in an age where more and more people are questioning what science or society has peddled to us as a "true reality". The followers of other world theories and conspiracy theories are steadily increasing. Conspiracy is a silly concept from my point of view. For, if anything, our well-known reality would be a conspiracy of society against the common man. But somehow it is so far that even if one believes in another theory, one is almost portrayed as a hater. In the past, such people were still being burned or tortured. There are other means available today, but I do not see much difference in our freedom with our own faith.

Is reality what we know, or what we see?

Because what we know is what we should know and what's been planted with us. And what we see *is* what we see because we know what we see. We see a tree and it's a tree because we *know* it's a tree. And we know it's a tree because we were once told and taught that. Even with this knowledge, a tree is a tree. For me, too, it is a tree, and it is very difficult for me to get out of these manifested basic ideas so that I can really look at a tree freely – and not only just see a 'tree', to understand that everything I regard as reality is the reality that society has created with all its facets.

Once we consider our perception then how do we see things? Do we all see the same things exactly alike or do we see things completely different?

Let's look at an object that lies ahead. When we look at it with the right eye, or the left eye, and with both eyes almost closed and then wide-eyed we will see that the object differently each time. It changed its place, possibly minimized in size and dimension. What is real if there is no firm picture in our own perception? How can we assume that someone else sees exactly the same that we do or sees the same colors, etc.?

If there is no fixed point in our own perception that represents the perfect truth of the view, then how can we assume that somebody else sees anything as we ourselves do? For this reason, everything is explained so that the explanation invoked is going to let us all see the same things?

Photography is also a mystery to me. I've been taking pictures for over 15 years and trying to capture life as I see it. But even photography is a bit absurd. Because I have infinite means to make something look completely different and as a photographer it is in my hands as I present something to the viewer. Nevertheless, I would go as far as to say that I am unable to photograph something in such a way that it is truly the picture I see and feel in the here and now in my conception of reality. I have a good camera with me wherever I go in order to be able to obtain a reasonable impression, or as close as possible to how I see them. Everything else is personally disappointing and often I prefer to keep a picture in my mind rather than holding an inferior, meaningless picture.

When I create an image as an artist, I realize that probably no one else will see this image as I see it and how I created it because everyone sees a different reality. Everyone takes in the world around himself or herself differently. If I am aware of that, it's still a huge chunk to accept that there is no ultimate reality and that none of what we see is as we see it. But for us it is exactly as we see it. Only we have enormous influence on how we perceive something.

When a younger child falls and has knee pain, it helps some children to blow the affected area and they feel better. Whether it's a kind of distraction, or the fact that you can comfort your child emotionally and then take away the pain at this level.

Should one then assume that it only works because it is a child that's perhaps too stupid to know that blowing actually does not take away pain, or is it just the reality of the child that allows something as simple as blowing to lessen the pain? Let's see how positive the whole thing is and how easy it is to shut off something like external physical pain when you're not yet clouded by a strange reality. Then one day it happens that the parents decide that their child is too old for such a thing and they tell him that it does not work at all and the child doesn't have less pain from blowing, that will change the child's reality in a sustainable way that is irreversible and you deprive the blowing of its previous ability.

Why should one do that if it is clearly beneficial in the child's reality? Just because it no longer suits their own reality, because they fear that the child in the eye of society will be considered to be underdeveloped, still believing in such childish things at a certain age? But is this childish or is it just another reality and, who tells us which reality is better?

I personally would rather take some air than painkillers, but even my reality was once bent to one in which, unfortunately, there is no real return. Although I have had several years of my life in which I have completely renounced any kind of medicine to be taken, this has taken a lot of mental strength, which, in my current state, I can no longer bring together for such things. At that time, it was another attempt to find out how far we'd got tarnished and I teased it out during an operation on my elbow without any anesthesia. What resulted were 3 horrible hours that painfully overshadowed everything that I had ever experienced and to which I was capable.

I have found that I do not want to indulge such an experience again and since then in certain situations I also fall back on medicine. Especially when it comes to avoidable pain. But I cannot say in general what it's like growing up mentally stronger. When I see tribes perform the most absurd 'surgeries' without any anesthesia and analgesics, and it's just the most normal event, unthinkable for us but completely normal for these people.

Apparently their reality does not reflect ours and even something such as pain is part of it to some extent.

Psyland is somehow a little game on my part with reality. Because for the small moments in which some people come here, they leave their reality and see a new one. One that is not less real or fake than theirs. Many people in this place have gone far beyond their known limits and there's something that you feel here which seems to be contagious when you go through certain rituals here. Because, for example, tattooing does not have much to do with today's tattooing as most tattooists here are or have confirmed that again and again although the physical process is not much different than in any popular tattoo studio in the world. Rather, it is what it means to come here and what the place and all that it brings affects people.

It's something that I find hard to describe and explain because it's outside of what most people see as their reality. Or what few have experienced for themselves. We try to create small modern rituals for the new generation of people.

We are a new tribe of people, and I do not consider it as a good and forward-looking thing to be too clingy to everything old. Let's take the tattoo. Clearly, the origin and tradition of it is beautiful, and I have endless experiences of being tattooed in a variety of traditional ways. But the whole is also a very laborious way and limits us in what we can do with our means today and within that constraint give us the observation and insight into the entire experience of all the tribes of all continents and all the ages would allow. We are a giant step ahead of what the previous tribes had in terms of possibilities. I would also just say that the tattoo artists used to have access to what they had been given the opportunity to do, and that in turn they would have tasted the fullest. And it does not matter if it's a tattoo artist, a shaman, a worker building houses and huts, painters, artists and so on. Every epoch is shaped by its means and possibilities.

As I said, I find it highly exciting and freaky what was created with limited means in history. But most of the time, it was not primitive at the time, but in fact more advanced and well developed. It is nice to know the story and to use it to the extent that you bring it to the current day and

82

your own reality in order to get the maximum out of it and not get stuck and stop developing. This often seems more like an excuse for not having to develop myself which in no way means that I do not appreciate rituals and significant events. But on the contrary, I believe that giving a ritual to a modern man in today's society, which is halfway within his own reality, will give him the opportunity to bring that experience into his everyday life.

For example, let's go to a shaman in the forest and go through an ayahuasca ritual like it was done 1000 years ago. So that's a nice and exciting great experience, but very alienating and even more so in such a moment. The experience gained from this is therefore completely different from adapting such a ritual to the modern man and his reality, thereby depriving him of the alienation of the moment. Thus, he can concentrate more consciously and unencumbered on what will hopefully enrich him for a long time in his life.

This hopefully changes his reality or at least gives him a fresh new perspective. And yes, sitting in the middle of the forest by a campfire, with shamanic drums and Icarus singing is represented in the fewest of us or ever even close to everyday life.

Just as little as being tattooed with a hammer and stick, or all sorts of other things can be spiritual things that many try because they can't cope with the reality of the new world. I firmly believe that this quest for a spiritual experience, or whatever you want to call it, truly discourages most people from living. Keeping from this creates their own reality. We read beautiful books and experiences of people who have suffered such things, or at least claim that such things have happened to them, but rarely do we meet such people on the street. Pretty much all of these ultra-spiritual people who have crossed my path and whom I have confronted with certain things or that I have observed in their being have not been nearly free. It seems nothing more than a masquerade, as it is simply hip and trendy these days.

On the other hand, I wonder why one should wait a lifetime for a spiritual experience, when all life is in front of one and can be enriched with simple little things.

And I've learned one thing: there are many things that you just cannot explain and either your opponent is open and brave enough to make a new experience or they're stuck in the safety of their present reality.

Unfortunately, growing up is not a great thing and in my opinion, it is the fault of the adults. Should not the adults prefer to help the children become more childish again? Wouldn't that be much easier and more fulfilling?

A child always laughs and is almost always happy. It does not wait for the one life-changing, spiritual experience in its life, but daily creates its own reality with the simplest things and with what lies ahead. It is a modern primitive who accesses everything he is capable of and does whatever is possible with it. Here he knows no boundaries in the sense that the external reality dictates to him. Everything can be used and used for everything. Whether it works then and continues to prevail is another question. And there is always a laugh in the face. Doesn't that sound like a better and more beautiful reality than the one in which most of us live?

Most people who know me, know that I do not really live in reality. And it is almost classified as a disease, because I thereby socialize very marginally. But how far do I live outside of reality if I accept that there is no perfect reality in that sense? When I acknowledge that the only reality is that which I create myself and in which I feel comfortable and can live in a way that the normal social reality can never impart to me. How is this worse for me than for someone who takes what you have in front of your eyes as it seems to be? For if we doubt everything and question everything, and everything we know loses its meaning, or its origin in meaning, what do we still see as reality after that?

For my part, I see myself more alive in reality than most people. At least once I am aware of my reality and how far I can move and live in it. However, I am also aware that my idea of reality is a long way from what most people might see as reality. But am I living outside the reality, or is it the others? Is there such a thing as an ultimate and only reality at all? Or are we able to create everything we want in our minds?

Does that make us socially ill and lonely? Yes, and we are regarded as mentally disturbed and you look at us as someone who does not live in reality even though we may see more consciously than most people of the reality that we live in and in turn, make our own. Apart from that, the word reality is already so fraught in our thoughts that it is almost impossible to form one's own judgment.

Whenever I write or talk about such things, I often have to listen to the fact that the use of psychedelics has alienated me completely from the world and I live in a surrealistic clouded world of thought. But how far can you say that? The effects of psychedelics are only for a short period of time and it doesn't let you see anything that you can't already see if you open your eyes and break out of your everyday thought scheme. Yes, the use of psychedelics has definitely changed my view of the world and has definitely played its part in doubting my reality more than before. But our social system and the manipulation of ordinary people were already well aware of it and are by no means dependent on the influence of any substances.

What should we see and what should we know? How far is this all pre-programmed and controlled? We live in a kind of matrix, because only through our mental influence and what is taught to us, what is real and what is not, do we see the world.

Again and again there are people who break this chain and show us a new reality. But how far are we bound by fears, beliefs and other obstacles to doubt these new truths?

Fear. Maybe also the fear that with the realization of a new truth, your life will change terribly and you will find no way back into a "normal" life and then you will be excluded from society. If one accepts this and then lives with more truth, might they also go in a lonelier and possibly unsatisfactory path? Those are the compromises that many people are unwilling to enter because there is no certainty that this gives you more freedom, happiness and a freer life. But sometimes the hope of freedom for some prisoners is more than they need to get through their time. And in my view, this seed of hope is usually enough already. Because without hope, one has given up a long time ago and then one will never make an escape attempt again, as the focus is lost.

To be led was once the easiest of all ways. Whether religion has taught reality, science, shamans, cult leaders, or just society. It is still the easiest way to live, to be guided. And if you follow all the guidelines, you will never be confronted with more serious, more complex situations that make you doubt your own complete existence, that one doubts his whole life. Or rather, the way one has led or is still leading one's life.

It is easy to acknowledge and co-opt the reality that is put at your feet, and I can imagine that many people find a certain fulfillment in it. But what happens when the day of realization comes and one has lost one's entire life? What if one realized one day what *could* have been? What life could have been if one had detached oneself from the template of the given reality?

Yes, then it is unfortunately too late and you begin to question your life shortly before death and / or after death and to repent. And that in turn can end fatally. According to Buddhist teachings, you then start to bother and torture yourself after death so that you're looking for a rebirth to start a better attempt, and then all that shit starts from scratch. I prefer to sizzle in hell.

Whatever you believe, the moment you face death, a lot will change and you will see your life differently. And wouldn't it be nice to be completely free in these moments because you really did what you always wanted to do?

People are afraid of death, but they should rather be afraid of what they miss in life.

To create one's own reality and to live in it, to blossom in it, to find a real life and fulfillment in it, is not an easy way. But it is a real way and at the end of the way you know that you are behind what you did and what you really wanted to do. At the end of the path, you may find your own perfect reality and the freedom that comes with it. Freedom is one of the greatest goals of every human and we will never find them in a fictive reality.

Let's compare the whole thing with a movie. Everything we see on the screen seems to happen, a full story, actions, dialogues and actions. But how much is real? Although we see it real on the screen and it was played in a realistic way.

But how much reality is behind it? Nothing. We see what we should see. We see what we should consider real. In a movie, we realize that what we see is not reality, but in our everyday lives, we take everything as it seems to be, without ever doubting it. If our life, as we accept it, is just a movie, then who writes the script?

Should not we take the pencil ourselves? Even take the camera or even be the main actor? Or should we go and have somebody else finish the movie?

Maybe we should burn down the film studio and go to the next forest to read a book.

Another beautiful aspect of how I personally experience the world consciously, or rather a conscious aspect, because it is not always very comfortable and beautiful: Normally, I am always barefoot and do not wear shoes. My own concern is to feel the world and to follow my path carefully and consciously. I'm not interested in bondage to the earth or any esoteric hippie stuff. My only concern is that every step I take is thoughtful and I feel where and why I am moving. Somehow it is sometimes quite exhausting, painful and painstaking. But I suppose so is the conscious life if you cannot just walk around step by step and protect yourself with shoes, no matter what lies ahead. Sometimes the path leads you next to the actual path, on a wall, in a meadow. It doesn't matter! Because who tells us where we walk, if not ourselves? Since I myself am barefoot, I go the way that feels good and not the way that makes the most sense, as in sense in the way of thinking, of how to get from A to B the fastest. I'm usually not fast, and my life is certainly not that much easier. But that's the least about it and the fastest way is rarely the best.

Our box is solid. Our box is as it should be filled. As it is shaped by education, society, school system and norms to explain our reality to us. But let's break this box and see reality from another perspective, then there is no turning back to a simple life, and much that was once significant loses all meaning and fulfillment. Because nothing we record through words or impressed experiences is of real meaning anymore.

Only our experience of breaking through our own mental reality and limit enriches us in a way that enables us to create our own, completely free reality.

For what is real, in an unreal world?

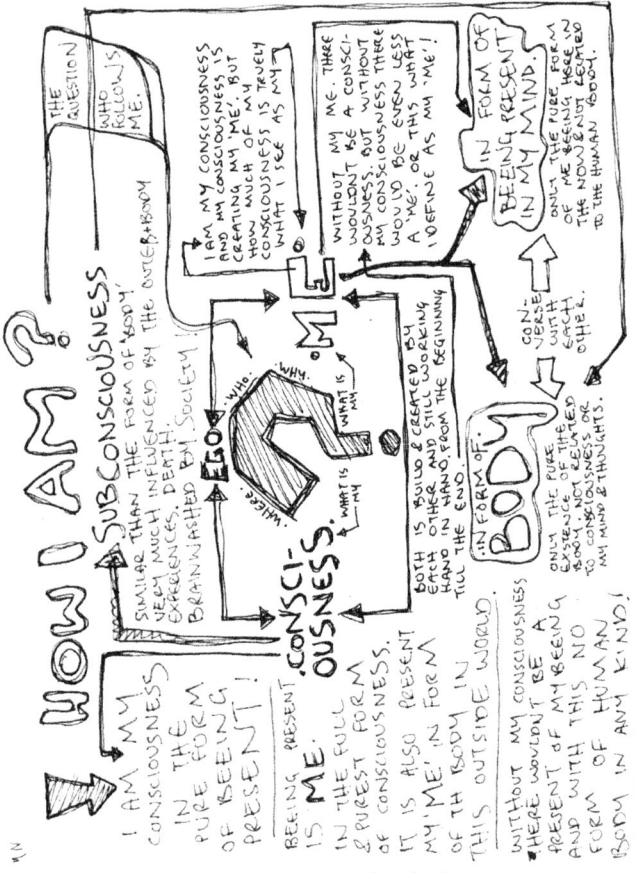

HOW I AM?

SUBCONSCIOUSNESS — SIMILAR THAN THE FORM OF BODY. VERY MUCH INFLUENCED BY THE OUTER+BODY EXPERIENCES, DEATH. BRAINWASHED BY SOCIETY.

THE QUESTION — WHO FOLLOWS ME.

I AM MY CONSCIOUSNESS AND MY CONSCIOUSNESS IS CREATING MY 'ME'. BUT HOW MUCH OF MY CONSCIOUSNESS IS TRUELY WHAT I SEE AS MY?

WITHOUT MY ME, THERE WOULDN'T BE A CONSCIOUSNESS. BUT WITHOUT MY CONSCIOUSNESS THERE WOULD BE EVEN LESS A 'ME'. OR THIS WHAT I DEFINE AS MY 'ME'!

IN FORM OF BEEING PRESENT IN MY MIND. ONLY THE PURE FORM OF ME BEEING HERE IN THE NOW AND RELATED TO THE HUMAN BODY.

I AM MY CONSCIOUSNESS IN THE PURE FORM OF BEEING PRESENT!

BEEING PRESENT. **CONSCIOUSNESS IS ME.** IN THE FULL & PUREST FORM OF CONSCIOUSNESS.

IT IS ALSO PRESENT MY 'ME' IN FORM OF TH BODY IN THIS OUTSIDE WORLD.

WITHOUT MY CONSCIOUSNESS HERE WOULDN'T BE A PRESENT OF MY BEEING AND WITH THIS NO FORM OF HUMAN BODY IN ANY KIND!

EGO
WHO.. WHY.. WHERE.. WHAT IS MY
WHAT IS MY
M.E.

BOTH IS BUILD & CREATED BY EACH OTHER AND STILL WORKING HAND IN HAND, FROM THE BEGINNING TILL THE END.

IN FORM OF **BODY.** ONLY THE PURE EXISTENCE OF THE BODY, NOT RELATED TO CONSCIOUSNESS OR MY MIND & THOUGHTS.

CONVERSE WITH EACH OTHER.

Everyone has a choice

As simple as it sounds, so complex is this issue.

For most people it takes a kind of breakdown in life, something like a near-death experience. Something that, overnight, confronts them with the transience of their life in a way that they have never experienced before. That can be of a different nature. Suppose you have a routine check-up with the doctor and he diagnoses a tumor or something else serious. The doctor sits in front of you and tells you that you only have six months to live. Such an experience will shake just about everyone out of life; or rather from the template they may have previously called life.

I am aware of this transience of life everyday, which is why I carry my countdown to me. And we all have a countdown, though not so visible most of the time, but we all carry our countdown to life with us. Because all of our earthly life within the human body is transient and we most likely have only one of them here to experience what we want to experience.I wonder how many people out there do something they really do not want to do. How many people work in a profession they do not like? Living in a city or apartment where you do not want to live. How many people out there live a life based on endless compromises? Because it may be offered, because you have a permanent job and get paid a good salary, because you live in a city just because you get to this place so much faster. Maybe because you are just used to living, as you are already alive and afraid to lose everything you have built up. But what did you build, what did you achieve, materially and socially? How far do you really go on to make all these so-called life enrichments or life goals?

Everyone has dreams, visions and ideas. But how many really start to live out their dreams? Act right and discard other things for it. Let's say someone works in a permanent job, for many years, with a secure non-terminable employment contract. He earns good money and can thus lead a socially regarded good life with a great car, a nice house, a holiday once a year, which just symbolizes a normal average good life.

Everything considered from the eyes of society, of course.

But suppose now that person has the idea, no, the dream, that one day he wants to do something absurd, or something else weird. Maybe even something quite simple which has become something absurd through the whole social life.

Whether it is a dream to open a flower shop or to paint pictures. No matter. We all have dreams. Or had dreams. At least as children, before we were dragged through all the social stupor that now tells us what life is.

Now how many people are ready to give up all this to pursue their dream? To do what you always wanted to do? How many are ready to listen to their innermost voice, to hear their hearts and to let themselves be guided by rational, socially influenced thinking? Yes, let's call it a "jump into the cold water", into the unknown. And yes, eventually you will lose everything you ever set up. Maybe you would lose this `beautiful life'. But how far is it a fulfilling life, living in eternal uncertainty, whether one could have realized his dreams? Would not one have had a fulfilling life if all were well? How far are people willing to live with this uncertainty? With the knowledge, to maybe never find out, never having lived their dreams, and for what? For the idea of a beautiful life, which in turn cannot be so fulfilling, if you keep in mind that you have quasi-unattainable dreams and goals in your head that you had simply let go.

And one day, when you are old, when you die, when you realize that life is over and the chance to do what you wanted to do, to do what you always dreamed of? How satisfied are you to look back on your life? How satisfied are you with the decision never to have made a decision?

Yes, I hope that most people get this realization much sooner. If this requires a near-death experience, a medical misdiagnosis, a serious accident or another stroke of fate that brings death and human transience into the eye. Then, it's still better than coming to this realization after it's too late if you've already let your earthly life get out of hand.

I have my countdown in sight. For a long time every decision I make tries to be based on my inner voice, my inner feeling. Far from logical, influenced thinking. Some experiences and situations are put to one's feet and yet many are inclined not to take these possibilities directly. Much has to do with fear, yes. Much has to do with the fact that you cannot let go and cling to the fact that you just do it another time.

If you have a countdown on you and then you look at the time. How far would it influence and guide us? How far would it change to choose our choice?

If there were no tomorrow, we would do it all today.

So yes, every person has the choice and that's exactly what I mean. Every choice and every decision has consequences, partly very hard, serious, life-changing consequences.

A conscious life will not always be the easiest, maybe not always the most fulfilling especially from the normal social point of view. But at the end of our earthly time we can look back, with the full awareness of having done exactly what we always wanted to do without compromises.

Yes, fear is the biggest weapon of the society to keep us in their templates so as not to break out. But how far do we want to lead our lives? How far do we want to guide each of our decisions? We actually have a lot of options. We have every choice, if we only want and get involved in the consequences.

What would be the worst thing that could happen and would it really be so bad that we'll never be able to get away from it? How hard can you fall? How deep can you fall if you know how far away the ground is? And no matter how many times you fall and how hard you fall. The feeling of getting up is always going to be great, and it will only make you even more solid in the fact that you have tried and continue to go through life.

Some things may be harder and you fall more often. But most of the things that make life worthwhile are not thrown in the shoes of society. For most great things in life you have to fight and fall. Fall often. Fall hard. But when you finally arrive at the destination, you appreciate it all even more.

Now we come to the choices. I have a firm belief that no matter what choices you make, no matter what consequences it brings, something wonderful can come of it. Something that would never arise if you just live in his everyday mask and let his life pass you by. Yes the hurdle can be huge. Outside of what you have ever dreamed.

Any dream can be unattainable for now. Yes, it must be virtually unreachable; otherwise it would not be a dream. But once you manifest it to a vision in your mind and decide to make that vision a reality, there is nothing that cannot be realized. Apart from that, you create your own reality anyway.

I find it a great example to compare life with a seed.

Let's say you get a seed as a gift, a seed, small, gray and puny. But it's a seed that carries something wonderful in itself, a flower, a tree, a completely new universe, and a kind of lifeform. Yes, this little seed will always be just a small seed, as long as you just let it lie there. If you are aware that you have only one seed and it is a seed that can blossom into the most beautiful plant in the world, then you will not just throw it in the ground and wait for a plant to grow out of it. You will eventually wait until you have enough time and energy to take care of this seed, to grow it properly, to water it and to seek a place with light and shelter. Yes, you will put love and energy in it and pull out a wonderful plant.

If we are now aware that this plant will become more beautiful and beautiful over the years, bigger and much more magnificent than we can ever imagine, will we wait forever until we sow this seed? Or will we try to adjust our circumstances to use it as quick as possible to enjoy its beauty and size as long as possible?

Probably yes.

Now let's take our life. Our life is this seed. We all carry it. We all have a life and a chance to make it what we want it to be. We all have the opportunity to grow our seed by the time we decide to sow it. Because to wait for the right time to come one day also means that we may have wasted many years in which this seed would have grown into a stately plant.

And that's exactly how it is with decisions. Why wait? Why waste time? To wait for safety and possibly the only chance one has to lose, or allow time to flourish around a wonderful cause. Once you have made a hard decision, with all its consequences and risks, you will be fully behind it and invest your entire heart and all your love. And what then will become out of life is to be seen.

I am the best example for this. Many people I meet that talk about an alternative life say that they do not have the opportunity and that in my case I have talent, happiness and so on and that's why it's so easy.

First and foremost I have to say that my path was easy and the decisions behind it were not easy. But without this choice, which I would make then and today, my life would never be the way it is today and it would never have been born from what has arisen. In my case, it was in the direction of tattooing and the longer I did that, the more uncompromising I became, or did I consciously choose which direction to go and eliminate everything else?

I watered my seed and from that I had the opportunity to cross borders that did not even exist before in this genre. If I just did everything halfheartedly alongside, today after 12 years I would still do the same thing I would have done 12 years ago. Monotony and habit and content with what you have. What you have in your own box. Yes, even the most beautiful box is just a box that can and must be broken because without it life loses in progress and development. And if the plant does not get any more water, it eventually dies.

Unfortunately, what qualities a single individual and how far it draws the fullest potential from it, can only be found out if it really goes its own way. Everyone has the choice. And every person should use it and let their hearts guide them to what they really want to do. And then something beautiful can come out of it. No matter in which direction, no matter which talent, which characteristics or ideas. Without water and without making the perfect choice, nothing will ever grow out of it.

We all have talents and fortunes and, unfortunately, few have the perfect time and energy to grow them as they could grow if they were less compromised. Many people are not even aware of their talents, because through the school system, through which we are traded, individual talents and interests are very quickly suppressed and dismissed. The adolescent is fed with all sorts of information and knowledge and is queried what is probably far beyond his own interests. And there's no time left for your own ideas and talents. After all, you are busy learning what you need to lead a good life later. And that's not so much in the eye of society. Or maybe very little and everything else is just a weapon to distract people and keep them away from their own thinking.

The fact is, many people have not discovered many of their talents at a very late age, and even less fully lived them out. And for those who discover and guess it, it usually only remains a dream to truly start doing more.

What does one have to lose already?

The only thing you can finally lose is a few years of his life, money and social status. But how far should one override this, if one lived completely free and consciously within this dream regardless of what period and what has finally become of it?

But to find out, there is only one way.

Is it the right moment that you wait for in life, or is it life itself, that you need to bend to the right moment?

Dreams.

One of my biggest dreams was to buy an old house with property one day. Something that I can transform and change, that I feel good about and that nobody can ever take away, something to create a place of freedom and creativity in, a place that reflects what I feel and think. I waited years and watched and waited for it until I found the perfect object. But the perfect object did not exist and it was my dream to create it.

One day I was there and my life was anything but solid and certain. I didn't even know exactly how it went on and when I was additionally terminated from my gallery, in which I spent 6 years of my life and was my little safe bubble. I was at the same time in the separation with the mother of my child, I fell in love with my wife, who lived on the other side of the world and I had more than chaos in my life. But this dream has been there for a long time and if everything goes down then it is right. While many would have said that would be the worst moment to do such a thing, they would probably be right and I would have saved a couple of very tough years. But I would never have what I have now and who knows if the right moment would have come or if I would still wait. I'm sure Psyland would not exist without that decision. Or at least not anything near as it is now.

Because even this seed is only sown and would be much bigger if I had gone this step years before.

Your dream comes to life when you start living your dream and in a dream everything is possible. For who is telling you what a dream is and what life is? Because your life is the biggest dream you can ever experience.

When you make your own choices, you will change your life and become whatever you always wanted. But to wait for the right moment and to let time pass is, in my opinion, not the way to go, because our clock is running, and with it every opportunity to live our lives. Living as we want and taking every opportunity to make our own choice.

There is nothing you cannot do. Only things you did not try.

Love is life

Love gives life. Life gives love. One of the most used quotes I use in my art, just the endless string of it, and the endless connection. One feeds the other.

First. When I use the word "love" in this context, I use it in a different context than most people interpret it. I do not speak of love in the sense of love for a person, family or a comparable feeling of love, sticking to one or more people. So never do I mean love between two people. Which does not mean that love between two people isn't something nice. But that's just another topic and it has nothing to do with how I personally use the word "love".

When I use the word love in my art, it is in a different context. I speak or think "love" in the sense of passion for something, sacrifice and the entire heart in one thing, meaning a life in which to pick up the seeds again. Yes, it takes love to make a plant grow from it. Love in the form of lifeblood, passion, time and energy that you put into something because if you do it solely out of the feeling of the heart, it will always be a beautiful thing. A bigger thing than we ever dreamed possible. That's exactly what I associate with the word love.

Love is more of an inner voice for me. An inner deep feeling that guides me through my life. I am aware that "love" is only a worldly word and never capable of what lies behind my idea of that feeling. Behind the feeling that leads my life, so to speak. This feeling that I always try to put over any thoughts. Yes, I try to be guided by love through my life and not by thought. Since any kind of thought, as already discussed, never reflects what I can and want to experience freely and unprotected.

I could also say that I let my heart guide me. But this is even more stupid, because an organ can guide us much less than a feeling. I personally would rather listen to an organ than to my brain. For our educated, logical thinking is the death of every free life. Over the years I have learned to completely disconnect my sense of love from thinking and to let myself be guided in difficult situations, intuitively and thoughtless.

Love and hate.

Yes, there is a lot of hate in my life although I want to explain that briefly. When I speak of "hate", it's not in relation to an individual or a single thing. When I say that I hate humanity, or the entire human race and what it does on Earth and how it behaves, that does not mean that I'm going so far that I hate a single person or wishing all people the worst. No, I wish they all would open their eyes and see life and love and water their damned seed. Unfortunately, that's not how society works and how it's built and yes, that finding fills me with hate in a way I can hardly describe. It is rather a deep sense of sadness when I see how people live and do exactly what they should do. Since time immemorial, I have been exploring social patterns of behavior and, unfortunately, it has been confirmed again and again. But this kind of hate opens my eyes all the more to what I think about life and the boundless infinite. Without darkness there would be no light, and without the night no day would exist. And so it is with love and hate. One always depends on the other. The more I love one thing, the more I hate in a way that attacks and threatens this love.

"Another wasted life" is a saying that I got in my

101

head when I see people who are so banal and waste their lives and do not even begin to go to the limit of their abilities.

Another point that leads me to a lot of hatred is the fact that I have tremendous love for some things in me and anyone who attacks any of these things in any way will not receive a good, nice feeling from me. For example, when I look at the tattoo scene and what has become of it, it's a thing that was once so great, a thing that once had so much meaning, a thing that I have sacrificed my life for and that is dearer to my heart than many other things. Now, when I see how everything turns out and a lot of people think they are jumping on this train to make easy money to get known or just because it's so cool now. Doing more with their actions and actions will only help to destroy this once beautiful thing. Well, then you should expect nothing but a kind of hate from people who have so much love behind them. I am well aware that I will not change this, but that is my attitude and my feeling and I will never hold back my emotions. Nowadays, it may even be more important than ever to really show where you stand and what you feel.

Well, in how far does love give me life or the other way around?

When I completely sacrifice myself and give everything for one thing, I give my whole heart and blot out everything else in a way, and then I'm convinced that something wonderful always comes out of it because it comes with love.

Nothing will give me more life, energy and motivation than to see something small come out of a small thing, "something small but with heart". And I

102

find that you always see if a person does something with total dedication, or does something because of money, reputation or fame. Perfect love for a cause cannot be bought, nor can it be anything that comes with it.

Commercialism.

To address that briefly, yes, even if you decide to do one thing solely out of love, it does not mean that you cannot earn money with it. But when does it start to spread from love to commercialism? I would say at the moment where you let go of your own actions from the feeling of love and adjust your business more with logical thinking in a way that is to draw more money, fame etc. from it.

In my life I have seen many people doing things out of love. The result is something wonderful and they became known. And with notoriety, there are also easy ways to earn much more money. And with easy ways to earn more money, many see little gaps they can exploit to market their stuff even better. To simply make more money with their cause than they would anyway.

In many cases, love falls by the wayside and changes perspective. It may keep many people from evolving, especially if you see that further development may mean fewer people like what they did before. And then you listen to the feeling of love and leave everything else behind. Or you adapt and continue doing what will bring you a profitable life.

But even that does not mean that you cannot earn well with a cause made out of love. Because if you can safely live on it and thus have more time and space to put even more love into what you really want to do, then this can be a nice thing and bring you even further.

But money can never guide love and never let it emerge from being guided independently and following its heart.

The complete surrender to one thing and the result is that is life. That's the life that makes up life, the potential that gives you life and helps you along the way. The greatest motivation for life is life itself and you just have to put love in it. Do not just accept every day as it comes and let time pass. No, live every day, with all your heart and your complete love in a thing that you really and completely want to do. For me personally, life is the only inspiration I have and need. Everything I've ever created is inspired by the life and love behind it.

Love is life ....

It is exactly like that because everything is directly related to a fulfilling life, to live and not just to exist. For to exist, in the form of a living organism, does not require a form of love. No motivation of love. No voice of the heart, which brings one forward and leads the way, none of this.

How far does this hang together in the roundabout I am describing? By being able to draw a life of fulfillment out of love for yourself, you begin to love your life so much more than you ever did. You begin to appreciate your life in a different way than before. His lifetime and the realization behind what you can do with this one life here. Once you have decided that you will not spend your time too much on unimportant things or on insignificant things, you will begin to see your life with new eyes, Out of eyes that show you life with so much more love, with so much more dedication, and with a boundlessness that comes with it when you have this realization.

The circle starts all over again, because with this new way of life, you will put so much more love and time into the things that are important to you and you will make fewer and fewer compromises. And the more often the whole thing repeats, the more radical you become in your actions, because the more life you draw from it, the more love you draw from it.

The circle closes and there is no escape.

Let go

It is one of my most important phrases in my mind, if not the most important. It's a term that has always accompanied me. Words that I recite in my head in certain situations over and over again. These two simple words have helped me so much.

Let go. Yes, from what? Maybe let go of everything, or perhaps, just let go of some things in the right situation. But, most importantly, a very purposeful letting go of thoughts because thoughts can be our biggest enemy. Thoughts like fear. Social prestige. Social glory. Fear of losing wealth, money and possessions. Fear of death. Fear of life. Everything is mentally influenced. Everything mentally guided by thoughts that were imprinted on us. Letting go of this can be one of the biggest tasks. A lifelong task.

Let go of his thought. Yeah, maybe his whole idea of the world and the life we know, because that is built on our pre-manipulated thought.

Anyone who is even looking for freedom must learn to let go. From everything you know and have experienced. To break a border, to go beyond it. To break this box and expand it. There is only one way. These are words that I always have in my head.

Let go.

That's my words, my feelings and my sensation. I say it to myself to remember what I do and why. Also by myself, because I too am the one who often wants to hold myself back. Let's call it the ego, the self, or even our thoughts that try to hold us back. I always try to let go and put my feelings above everything else.

How often do you face a decision at any given moment in your life, no matter what nature, and the thoughts are to lead you immediately? The thoughts carry you and always lead you through life, the thoughts that are nothing more than a projection of society that tells you what is right and wrong. To let go of it means to listen to your heart completely. Listen to the love, to what gives you this inner voice, this feeling and what says, what is really close to your heart. Love above fear. These simple words, even more simplified in the word, let go.

Letting go of everything we know and feel. Of everything that has guided us because then we have a new world at our feet. An entire universe or just a little nudge in the right direction to what you feel as life itself. Nobody can tell us what life is; no one can explain to us what it really is. It is something we have to experience through our own experiences, pure new experiences outside of our already existing knowledge. To do that we have to let go and accept how ignorant we are.

Sometimes it cannot hurt to consciously let go of something to challenge yourself. My greatest challenge in this regard is currently my transformation into a female body. The whole thing is a bigger challenge than I ever thought and it has many reasons. My main reason is to let go of our imprinted gender role distribution.

Like most, I was raised gender based. I have wandered through society with the duties of a man and the pressure to fulfill them. I also do not think it makes a difference, man or woman. Both sides are probably similar in there and try to maintain this image, also with the assumption that the opposite sex is so expected. A woman wants a real male and a man wants a real female. That again brings us back only deeper in this role. But we all are influenced from early on, that it is incredibly difficult to break such a scheme and mock and expose the few who dare.

For many years, I did not feel like a man in myself anymore, although not as a woman either but rather somewhere in between. I quickly became aware of my role as a man, and I played it the same way like the most, so it was almost an impossible thought to let go of it. But some things just need some time and maybe I was just not ready for such a big step. I feel just as little a woman as I feel as a man by now. Still, I still feel much simpler and more comfortable in my outward role as a man. Thirty years in society have probably shaped me more clearly than I want to admit it myself.

Right now, both of my gender roles are like game

characters that I put into when I go to the outer world. Before that, I was never aware of it as I am now. I simply lived as a man before I did not completely analyze why I do certain things and why not.

For example, I've never been a big lover of fashion and clothing, etc., but I've always found women's clothing much more interesting and beautiful than what men have. However, I never thought of putting on women's clothes. And it was never completely important to me with the clothes and the look. Say, no matter how much I care, what and how I was dressed, I still cared that my male image was destroyed. I should also suggest that for a few years in my life, I had worn my clothes inside out to make my little silent protest against what embodies fashion and outwardness in our society. Now, in hindsight, I have to smile about it myself. But back then I felt that it was a big step for myself. Yes, I was still young and naive when I look back on it. By the time I thought I could make a difference and change, and a lot of meaning.

At the time, it was more rebellion than letting go, more provocation than freedom. But I suppose that is all part of the development and as long as you do not take yourself too seriously you will hopefully find a way to let go of it and one day to laugh at yourself.

Yes, no matter what I was. I was a man and mostly felt that way too. Or can one say that until now I had no idea of a different feeling or became acquainted with it? Only much later and in out-of-body experiences did I come to know and appreciate it. From there it took years to even fully understand what and how I can integrate this into my outer life.

Now I have been living more consciously with it for some years and I try to let go more and more of my male image. I wear skirts and dresses and try not to give myself as a woman or as a man. Still, I have to say that it is still a long way from completely releasing my male ego. Which has moved me to the subsequent and, in my view, seemingly meaningful de-cision.

Maybe it is not enough to break the male ego by trying to live more freely. Maybe this requires a more radical step and that means that for the first time you have to completely give up your masculine identity and live a few years as a woman. The whole of course based on the externality there, as already mentioned, I feel inside not really gender-related. The whole thing will eventually and hopefully have a big impact on what I'm going to experience with my experiences and the complete break of my male ego. It is one thing to think and feel something and to go to a completely different, irreversible, external transformation step. I have lived through this several times in the past and always learned to appreciate it.

So, it's one thing to put on a dress and another go through a transsexual transformation, which involves taking female hormones and possibly performing some surgery to change my outward image to a degree that there is no turning back to a real man. I think only then will I be able to live free from gender roles.

I will definitely not try to become a woman, even if I may look like this. My motivation is solely the experience of this transformation and what I call letting go.

Let go of the man.

Where all this leads me, I cannot say right now and it does not matter in my eyes. Because every experience brings us forward and the harder it is, the more you can pull out of it. My decision to have 2 fingers removed years ago, for example, ranges in a similar area. Of course, I was clearly concerned with the aesthetic part of this change, with so many factors attached to it that it was a very long and hard process of my life. It was something I carried for about 9 years. Until the day I broke this border. When I let go of something that is very important to me, just to prove something to myself? Challenge accepted!

My hands are what was and is most important to me from my external body, as it's my tools to bring out most of what's in my head. So it was a tricky game with the fire you could say. But considering that I've had that in me for so many years and even started the "last years of my old hands", where I would deliberately do things without the fingers to find out how much it would affect and discriminate me, it's not so much at random anymore.

It is my daily reminder that I do not have normal hands because I do not want to live a normal life and just as much as I do not want to do it in the normal way. It was another step to break myself and give me courage to do things differently.

Likewise, it was of course a big social step, because I was aware of how this affects the normal person and for me to let go of another step. If I am labeled as sick, then so it may be. Because if it is sick to want to feel free and want to live more freely, then I like to accept this disease for what it brings me.

Maybe it just means letting go of a healthy life because, what is considered to be a healthy life for most, is in my opinion, more than questionable. But who asks me? I am mentally disturbed and ill anyway.

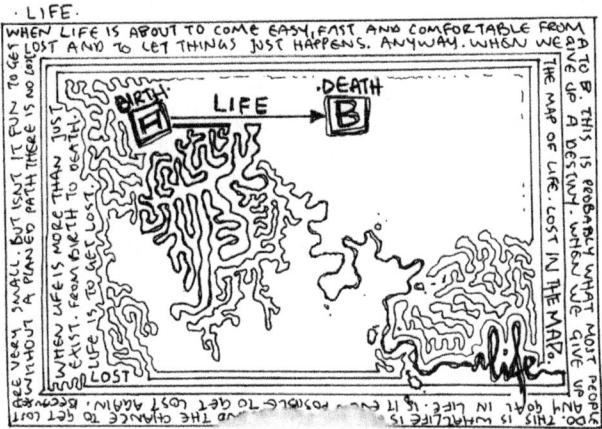

· LIFE ·
WHEN LIFE IS ABOUT TO COME EASY, FAST AND COMFORTABLE FROM LOST AND TO LET THINGS JUST HAPPENS. ANYWAY. WHEN WE...
BIRTH — LIFE → DEATH
B. THIS IS PROBABLY WHAT MOST PEOPLE... THE MAP OF LIFE. LOST IN THE MAP.
ARE VERY SMALL. BUT ISN'T IT FUN TO GET LOST AND TO... A PLANNED PATH THERE IS NO... WHEN LIFE IS MORE THAN JUST EXIST. FROM BIRTH TO DEATH. LIFE IS TO GET LOST.
LOST
GOD. THIS IS WHAT LIFE IS... IN LIFE. IS IT EVEN POSSIBLE TO GET LOST AGAIN?. BECAUSE... AND THE CHANCE TO GET LOST

Am I stupid enough to think that I'm wise? Or am I wise enough to know how stupid I am? How little I actually know about life? How little I know of what I do not know? And I'm not talking about the things I do not know, but about which I know they exist. I'm talking about things I do not even know I do not know. Do I know what I should know or what I want to know? In my eyes, I have accepted that I know nothing and do not want to know anything about what already is earthly knowing. How far does it affect my real life? Not really. Even if I carried all the earthly knowledge in me, I would be ignorant of what's behind it. For my part, I have acknowledged that earthly knowledge and ideas are useless. Of course there are things that are interesting, that concern me, that I inform myself or who investigates it. But I have acknowledged that they mean nothing to me at all and that they do not change my idea of reality.

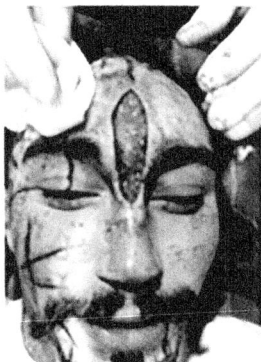

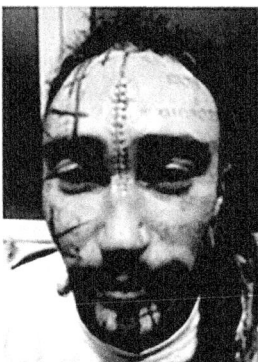

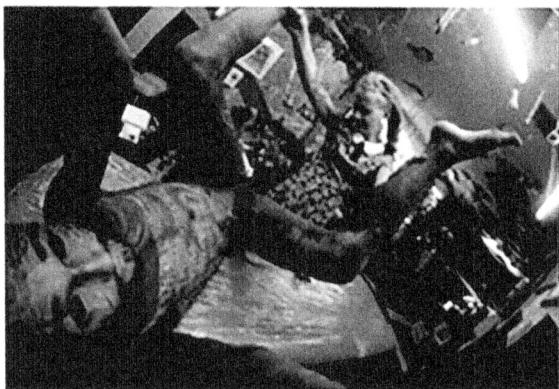

Once you realize how important it is to let go of any kind of belief and knowledge, you will be able to break new horizons. Once you acknowledge and target boundaries, you arrive at points in your life where you have to act against any kind of human mind. Yes, where you have to let go. If others say that I have lost all sense, then I like to approve and stand proudly behind it. For the intellect and spirituality are only worldly concepts of people who have never crossed a border. I mean People who hang deeper in the template than they will ever admit, or want or do. Who defines what is crazy and disturbed? Is it our society or every person for itself?

How far do I have to break away from society to find my own individuality? How far do I have to let go and accept that I cannot be accepted anymore?

Yes, this little word. This single word is a word that has strengthened and guided me in so many situations, such as in rituals or other moments where I have broken my own limits. In these moments where I have acted against any kind of social, logical thinking, in these moments where I have repeated and repeated this word in my head. Where I had to give myself a kick in the butt to really let go. It was and is not always easy. Yes, it can become a life's work. Especially if you know your thoughts and their origins and you have to jump over your own mindset. Let go of your own self. But if you realize that your ego is heavily manipulated for the most part by your social past, how far is it your own self? Where is this true idea of your own self? How far do I really have to let go of everything, including my own self to find out? To find my own self, my own idea of what life symbolizes and reflects for me.

113

We all have negative events and experiences in our past. But how far should we hold on to it? How far will the past bring us forward, or will it just stop us? Holding back to really experience new things? Sometimes you have to break away from the old to make room for something new. I also like to draw a line and walk over it. To take the past as a border and to leave it behind with the step beyond is definitely not always easy and it needs several attempts from time to time, but should you give up just because you failed the first attempt? Or should it be seen as a motivation that drives you to try it until you can really let it go, until you're ready to leave something behind that will not enrich you in the future?

How far are we if we do not manage to let go? How far do we live free and pure if we do not let go?

And even if we do it and create our own box, is it nothing more than a new box and a new perspective? A box from which we have to let go just like everything else to get ahead. To go further and define our lives in a way so we can find freedom in it is found within the internal or external form.

Because to live free, in the form of "free in the head", or to let go of what we know, and also be "free" that is true freedom; the feeling of freedom. And isn't that exactly what defines life in this outer world?

DEATH - OR LIFE

In what way are these two things rooted together and how far do they affect our everyday lives?

If you say that death is a long way off and has no bearing on you, I would say it still guides and influences you at the very least subconsciously, because most of us unconsciously "feel" death as a permanent presence. The denial of this will in no way free us from it, but will only keep us more aware than it already does.

How aware are we of death and what is our idea of it?

The idea of what happens to us in the afterlife is something that has always been pondered and speculated about. It is perhaps the biggest mystery of mankind.

But none of what we know about it is based on our own experience. None of this is actual free knowledge. It doesn't mean that you can't have an idea of it or that you can't speculate, or believe and think about what might happen to one after the human shell loses its life.

For me, the concept of death is one of the most beautiful topics when I talk about life because without death, there would be no life at all. Without death, we wouldn't even be aware of the existence of life.

But what is life and what is death?

How far is our inner world connected with the external? And how far can we lean out of our box to look at it objectively, and describe what our idea of death is and what maybe happens to us afterward? What is our idea, without being biased by what has been drummed into us from childhood?

For death has always been one of the greatest means of keeping simple people alive. Any kind of religion or belief system uses this very idea and the anxiety involved to keep its believers and followers in chains.

Let's talk about religion first using no more and no less than one of the many belief systems that we know, use or avoid.

I find it incomprehensible how people accept something so banal as a belief system. And I mean, even if you believe in something like God, a higher power, or something that has created us. Even if one has created something earth, man and all life believe in. Just the fact that all this has something to do with some kind of belief system, which in turn is supposed to guide you through life simply and calmly, is simply incomprehensible to me. Religion.

I was raised Catholic and was thus led by Catholicism through school. However, I was aware at a very early age that the idea of God is not something I would ever make friends with. Maybe I just didn't like the idea that I would most certainly end up in hell and understanding that believing was easier than becoming a good Christian.

Even more absurd than any idea of God, I found the idea absurd that there was such a thing as God, and an institution like the one of the Lord, that took the Church out, to claim to represent and speak for him. That did not make any sense at all. But who was I to defend myself against it at such an early age? I did the best I possibly could but eventually, I had to go to religious education as well as others and at an early age, I had to go to church.

Because this belief was imposed on me as a child and I was baptized, later on, it was not even possible for me to leave the church. I had to wait until I was 18 to legally separate myself from the whole thing. So much for how bold the Catholic Church is still represented in our system and how far parents can push their children into something, tying them up whether this belief system is their way or not.

And the Catholic Church is in my eyes one of the most unscrupulous, brutal and despised institutions that exist on this earth.

If we look through the entire history of the Church, how many people were cruelly killed and tortured? These outrages occur even today, always and again coming public as priests are discovered to be molesting children. And in countries such as Africa, where overpopulation and starvation are the order of the day, condoms are banned and magnificent churches built instead of helping people. I think we all know of more than enough incidents from the past and especially from our time that are just not justifiable. Nevertheless, the cross of the church is found everywhere in Europe. Actually, an unreasonable impudence if we think about it properly.

Now I'll go for a quick look as I always find a nice comparison. Especially in Germany, the subject of the swastika is a very special one. I do not want to go further into details about the swastika now. For those who do not know what the original meaning of this sign was and is, you should just Google it for a moment and find out by yourself because ironically, we talk about religions, politics, and for weeks about Hitler and the World War in school, but that this sign has a completely different meaning is by no means ever mentioned.

I guess we should not know too much.

In Germany, it is forbidden to use this symbol, no matter in which context. Even if you are a Buddhist and it is one of the most important signs in your religion and we seem to enjoy religious freedom. So no distinction is made which of these symbols you may use in which context just because they are similar in appearance.

The reason: Because of all the misdeeds that happened in World War II. Even so, does it make sense that this symbol is then banned in this context, or would just the necessary enlightenment behind it make more sense, instead of just meaningless blindly prohibiting anything that looks even similar?

And when we see it that way, I wonder why the Catholic Cross of the Church is not prohibited, because under this sign significantly more people have died to this day than died under Hitler, and at least as cruelly, if not worse. As we look at the history of the Church, we quickly find that many innocents have believed in an intuition that is supposed to be led by God and that wills you to live their will.

You should not kill and love your neighbor as yourself. BUT:

If your neighbor, for example, is gay, then you should kill him. I read the Bible at the age of 19-20 to obtain my own picture of how the Christians build their livelihood. And the entire work is repeatedly a contradiction in itself and has some very heinous passages. No wonder that Hitler was a Christian, and so again the picture blends. Let's just say that without Christianity and God the Second World War would have never existed.

Incidentally, under Hitler's regime, it was forbidden to talk about the true origin of the swastika and to spread it. Quite questionable, that today we are still on the same level.

Christianity was the beginning of many evil misdeeds, murders, sexism and much more. It was the beginning of racism and the subsequent killing of other races/people of other faiths. As far as the eradication of entire cultures and tribes by the Christian colonies and the prohibition under capital punishment introduced with it, that in many cultures, islands and tribes the locals were no longer allowed to live out their own culture and religion but were virtually forced to the Catholic faith.

We know everything, right?

However, the damn Christian Cross sometimes hangs in German classrooms and many public places. Especially in Europe and the people are too blind and too stupid to see what is behind everything.

I have another little story about that. When my daughter Maya was in kindergarten, and it was not a church-founded or religious kindergarten, I had painted upside-down crosses on her lunch-can. At that time I had joked that it was to protect her from evil Christians. Whereupon Maya's mother then received a warning from the kindergarten staff, as the crosses would offend the other children.

3-4-year-old children cannot even pronounce the word "religion". If that is not ridiculous then I don't know what is. Where it seems no problem if a child, in turn, carries a Christian cross around his neck on a chain.

It begins this early imprinting upon people something like a belief system, presented as completely natural, normal and unquestionable. It is simply accepted and not further considered in what way it stands for itself as a human being or for humanity in itself as something positive. In the past, religions were far better at guiding people than they are today. Nevertheless, it is still not completely abandoned and used widely in our system. Many people, e.g. Believing in God still believe in what science tells them. Which, in return, is a 100% contradiction to what the church claims to be what God is and has created. I do not understand how to believe in two different theories without being confused or believe in anything that is told or imprinted on us by other people.

Enough of this digression, what I mean by this is that almost all of us, as children, have been influenced by an idea of faith and quite clearly with the belief, too, of an idea of death that we may no longer fully believe, but that we still carry in ourselves. The manifestation of the concepts, God, heaven, hell, devil, are very concrete examples in my case.

Despite my completely self-created worldview on life and death, I carry impressions of concepts and feelings in me, which were given to me on the way at a very young age. This sip of Coke as I like to call the whole thing, I carry very little of it in my already very dilute canister of water because getting something completely out of oneself is impossible in my eyes. But we already talked about that.

When I heard that someone wanted to baptize their children, I always have big arguments. The statement that the child can decide later whether it wants to quit the church or stay is not so easy to answer. For how far is the child still free to decide for themself if they have already been given manipulated ideas? It's something that can never be erased from your system. If we know that, how far are you ready to say that you let your child decide freely? If one has already decided what is to memorize in his mind irreversibly. Because that's what you finally do with it.

We as parents are the biggest influence for our children and set the most deep-seated ideas. Or, the moment we deliver our children to kindergartens, schools, etc., we also give up this control and let people guide and shape our children, people who themselves have been shaped the same way, trained and educated. They shape innocent children into people who function socially. Because that's not exactly what it's about, to function as a human being in society.

I also do not think that this happens on a conscious level, but that these people have in turn been raised and influenced in the same way that in their present state are convinced that they are doing something good. Yes, even that they give the young adolescent something good. They prepare for a better life, for a great life in society. To what extent do they find perfect fulfillment in it is out of the question and in how far they give something good to the adolescent? Now one wonders what all this has to do with death. A lot, since we are influenced by early childhood of exactly those people who impose religions and other belief systems on these, and us in turn, provide an idea of death.

What does one carry in oneself for an idea of death?

And then I meet people who tell me they do not believe in anything. Nothing. What is nothing?

Personally, I do not believe in anything, or I do not believe that anything is real, or better off pressed I believe that pretty much everything is possible and so I just don't want to limit myself to a single option. So basically, I believe in everything and not in anything. Even if nothing is real and only real in my imagination, I still have quite a few ideas about many things.

For many years, I had no idea what would wait for me after death. But the idea that there is nothing was almost more strange to me than many other concepts. Even if I do not know what's outside of my box, I'm still not assuming that there is no "outside" of my box. For then I would again limit myself to the existence of my box and limit myself again in their limits and possibilities.

This word `nothing' alone is very strange. If we consider what is already known exists. How should there be 'nothing' and 'nothing' somewhere? If somebody says he thinks then nothing would happen, does he have the perfect conviction that there really is nothing or of what exists after that? Or does he simply have no idea or belief of what might be after that?

And I mean it's nothing negative to be unaware of what comes next. But to believe an emptiness of nothingness exists is very ridiculous in my opinion. Apart from that, what is nothing? Because even in the afterlife a nothing would be something in a certain way and would eventually be perceived.

Just as there is no 'nothing' on our earth. Any kind of teaching is filled with molecules, atoms, and other things. And just because we are usually not able to see this filled doctrine with the limitation of our human abilities does not mean that we have a perfect emptiness. There is no such thing as an empty space, nor will there be a void of nothing in my eyes as we move out of our bodies.

What would be the meaning of life if death were "nothing"? Is it possible to define life without death? Somehow death is always present and keeps many of us within own limits or borders.

The term death is a word that already carries so many negative attachments that it is far from a good term to define what I see behind it. If anything, 'death' is just another way of being for me. Again, life is nothing but another form of existence.

Body and consciousness

How far are body and consciousness connected and how far do you believe that one without the other does not work?

I can answer this question very well, at least for myself. I define my self far more by my consciousness than by my external human shell. Definitely, my outward form also influences my consciousness. But still, I believe that my consciousness controls my outward behavior. Say, when I speak or think of myself, then always in the context of my consciousness and not in the context of what we consider outwardly as human.

Who am I? I am Marc.

If only it would be so easy to answer that question that has always accompanied me.

Well, yes, I am my consciousness.

But who or what is my consciousness and how do I define my consciousness?

As my consciousness embodies something like existence, my subconscious embodies something like the outer shell of it. I suspect that the subconscious is strongly influenced by the external. Maybe even completely created by the outer world. So when I speak of my consciousness, it is always about my pure consciousness. The coupling and interaction between the two of them are more than conscious to me and perhaps even more obvious than the ego.

While I suspect that my consciousness could definitely exist unconsciously and that the subconscious mind exists subconsciously until it finds a way to actively intervene or, by understanding that you can work with it to get it into your consciousness. Thus, gaining subconscious control, which in turn brings it out into the external world, or at least nearer it. But yes, the subconscious is our coke and can never be removed once it has been emptied into our consciousness.

How far is my consciousness my self?

This question came to me when I wrote the first version of this chapter, whereupon I have spent a lot of time in my thoughts to find an answer for them at least for me.

How do I define my ego? What do I mean when I use the word I to define myself.

I am Marc.

Let's start at the bottom. The word "I" is already so afflicted that the statement of the ego is already connected with the external human body. So when I speak of my ego, I always speak in the form of existence and not in the form of the body. I define my ego about the pure form of my existence. Regardless of what my ego represents in the form of the body. This already roughly indicates that my ego can exist without any connection to my human body.

In my case, I differentiate my ego into an 'I' in the form of pure existence and an 'I' in the form of the human body whereby both forms of the ego are in a kind of mutual interaction. Since my body could exist neither without my existence, which in turn is clearly shaped in a way by my outer shell and its influences.

Whether and how far my existence is connected with the existence of my body I can not answer for myself. I do not carry any information that points me to a past life or an earlier existence of myself. Likewise, I have so far no experience in which I could conclude.

However, I would not claim that the pure existence of my body then brought my existence into being. Eventually, even the very existence of my being has created something like an outer human shell to allow my ego to interact in this world.

Without my ego, my consciousness would not exist.

But without my consciousness, there would be even less my ego. If both are in turn connected, let's call this "bridge in between our ego", joining our interaction of consciousness and our ego in the pure external form. For many people, the ego is the biggest reason why they no longer bring their full consciousness into their bodies, or into their external life. Eventually, this was only created by our subconscious to guide us, as we are to live outwardly as human beings.

It could be argued that the subconscious mind is something like a filtering system of the system, which in turn uses the ego as a filter to control what and how a person perceives things in his environment and how he behaves. But that's just one theory of many.

By the word ego, I do not mean the same thing as self-reliance or selfishness. And once again, it's just shitty to use words that already have a burden, but we've already had that topic and no word is completely unloaded, and in the end, I'm using something similar.

Self-confidence is probably a very strong trait that makes people go further than their ego ever lets them trust. While your ego keeps you in a template in which you cannot, for example, become or be allowed to get dirty. Because you may be so good at one thing that you carry the belief that there is no better way than what you know. But a healthy self-confidence lets you crawl through the mud and roll through the mud. As long as you find ways to develop even the most perfect thing. If there are no limits, there is no final solution to a cause.

The day you believe that you cannot learn anything is the day your ego gains the upper hand. From that day on, you will probably not develop anymore. No matter in what form.

So you should generally differentiate between ego and self-esteem and never let your ego stop you from developing.

While one's ego says one is the best, one's self-confidence will tell you that you are good enough to be better. Which in return gives you enough room for further personal development, no matter in which frame and whether inside or outside.

To summarize it again roughly;

I am my consciousness in the form of existence. My being is my ego in the form of full pure consciousness and embodies my ego over the body on the external world. Without my consciousness, there would be no existence and thus no ego in external human form.

But what does all this have to do with death?

Personally, I have taken the greatest knowledge of death from my out-of-body experiences. Since childhood, shamanic rituals, the 'Rite of Passage' of different tribes and other body modifications, which in return represented certain events in the respective tribes and cultures, have fascinated me.

Pain has always been one of the greatest companions to most of these rituals. Even if it is not in the foreground, it is still part of it and always present. It is part of the border, part of the fear and the hurdle to break. Rituals are nothing more than a way to break the box.

Each of these rituals is a kind of border crossing in which one must completely let go of everything we know. Because even pain is just an emotion and a charm of the outer human shell and with the right mental focus, a limit that you can very easily control or exceed. Or maybe better formulated, which you can at least very easily accept and live through if you are ready to do so.

Pain is nothing, in proportion to what you can get for it. And that applies to many things in life. Mostly everything starts with destruction. To develop myself humanly, I first have to destroy my ego. This can happen on many levels, but for me, rituals have always been a nice way to confront me with something like this. Especially when it comes to things like pain, which the human being tends to avoid out of natural instinct.

Pain is a purely external emotion and sensation.

How far are we, as humans, mentally willing to accept this pain completely and to accept certain things? Well, in extreme situations we humans are capable of anything. When it comes to our lives, we can live weeks without food. Defying low temperatures, absorbing extreme loads of unbelievably suffering and pain to survive.

But how is it when you are fully aware of the event and get involved in a situation that brings enormous pain? If you can stop at any time and are aware of it,

Then how far can the right focus be placed?

With the right drive and the perfect belief that there are no limits, the feeling, the emotions, and the substances that the human body excretes in such situations.

The mental states that I have achieved in the very early stages of my life through a variety of rituals have influenced me more than any external influences.

All my first mind-expanding experiences have been purely ritual-related.

As with one of my first rituals, which was the splitting of my tongue. And I'm not talking about how it is done today, which is more like a surgical procedure than any kind of ritual. Of course, the result is nicer, the healing easier and the attachment as well. But the mental modification almost does not exist.

My tongue was split with a scalpel the first time shortly after I turned 18. Without any anesthetic or other aids. Only my mental will was the weapon against the pain. It was one of a total of 3 divisions of my tongue. Including the long healing phase, in which you could tear your tongue apart every morning. The mental preparation alone did not let me sleep for days before that along with the uncertainty about being mentally strong enough to go through such a ritual.

But in the end, there is only one answer to that question, and that is in the moment of experience. The moment the scalpel lies on your tongue. I have always loved to go and enjoy these steps, the step to go inwardly and not because of the pain, not at all because of the pain but the fear and uncertainty of whether one can endure the pain and can earn his modification.

I have never been, and am still less, a friend of pain these days. But the freedom to go beyond these limits yourself, even break your box, is it what appeals to me the most.

What is then already transient pain with what you can receive inwardly and outwardly for it?

From this ritual to my first complete out-of-body experience, which I had at about 21, many rituals have come in many different forms and through them; I have become acquainted with very absurd states of my mind. Although I had never experienced a complete separation of my consciousness from my body, I had achieved very similar states in which I stood in a kind of limbo between the two.

I do not remember exactly when it was, but I remember vividly and emotionally the situation and experience I had when the first time my consciousness completely broke away from my body. In a way that I'd never experienced before. We had worked on my forehead to apply an implant and I have traveled back and forth between unconsciousness and consciousness several times.

It was also in the early years of my life that I completely rejected any kind of medicine, addictive substances, or substances that affect my body in any way, probably the most mentally strong time of my life.

But that day I came to the limit of what pain I could endure with being fully conscious. So my body has been trying to eliminate my consciousness by unconsciousness. Through breathing and focus,

I had nevertheless kept myself conscious for a very long time and tortured myself through the procedure. Just before we were done and I was about to faint again and I had no strength left. Whether it was because of the already long exhaustion or the fact that I knew that it was almost behind me, I can't tell.

But at that moment I could not hold my consciousness anymore and something occurred, so surreal that had never happened before in my life.

I could completely let go for the first time.

I have lost all feeling from my body, any grip and any control over my body. But my consciousness was completely normal and even clearer than the hours before it came this moment when I had completely dissolved, where I almost wandered out of my body for the first time.

It's very hard for me to describe because it's something that did not exist in my box before.

It almost took my consciousness, my existence, my ego out of my head and it only became clear to me when I flew over my own body. I looked at the room from above and realized how aware everything is. How everything is from who I am and what I think and from what I call consciousness since that day. From what I am, what I see, feel and perceive myself. It was just unbelievable and the few minutes that I spent in this state were and still are one of the most influential experiences I've ever made and have completely redefined my worldview, most of all, in terms of death.

The day I became aware of my self.

The understanding of what I had after that of myself was different. And it was an understanding of one's own unbiased experience. It was unencumbered free knowledge. With this understanding, over the years, I began looking for rituals and events in which I was and can reach such states of mind, thus anchoring my own notion behind them more and more in my consciousness. I became addicted to this experience and state of mind.

I quickly realized that my limits are very wide and it is not enough to put a little toe over it to catapult my consciousness out of my body, which in turn has led to very absurd rituals and experiences. But every time you cross a border, the border moves and it becomes more difficult to cross this new border. If you live this out over many years, that's just the simplest explanation for why I've done certain things in my life that are totally incomprehensible to many.

For me, they were always just a means to an end.

Many years later, through other shamanic rituals, I got access to psychedelics. By that, I mean solely to use for the achievement of consciousness-expanding states, for rituals or healing purposes, just as they have been used in shamanic practices for thousands of years. The use of pure psychedelics has shown me very quickly how easy it is to bring one's mind into a mind-expanding state with the right usage and dose.

I'm just talking about a mind-expanding state, not a state of complete separation of the ego and the body.

As with everything else, I quickly started pushing to the limit. Or let's say, far beyond the borders.

If even a normal dose of LSD expands my consciousness so much that I blur any limits of the box, then how must it be to go beyond this limit? Similar to my other rituals, where I put the limit to myself very far away and am completely aware of everything. Psychedelics, along with my other shamanic rituals and experiences, were another very formative achievement in my life.

I do most of my deeply developmental psychedelic travels on my own. As with body-related rituals, I love being naked. The clothing offers us protection and hiding places, and thus to feel completely vulnerable I remove the armor and thereby become vulnerable. Personally, it makes it easier for me to take off my human shell as well.

Over a few years, I have become more and more involved in the matter and dosed my trips even higher. Until one day I had my first overdose. In this case, I hate to call it an overdose, because you can't really overdose on pure LSD 25, purely from the physical toxic effect. Well, yes, I've had many trips before, in which I had such intensity that it was very easy to travel back and forth between my consciousness and the outer world. At that time, I called it an overdose, which then manifested itself as a kind of much more serious LSD trip in me and since then, I have taken LSD in normal doses very rarely.

With a super high-dosed LSD trip, a serious LSD trip as I call it, it is very easy for me, or it is inevitable to leave the body in a way that has happened to me with only a few other rituals. And the special thing about it is that after about 5-8 hours I need to find myself in this kind of state of consciousness, my consciousness completely out of my body but unlike DMT, where it puts me in a surreal dimension.

It is a perfect resolution of my self from my body, partly interacting with the world, quasi from a different angle, from which I can partially view my body, which is in a kind of sleep state, almost the separation of my physical ego from my ego in the form of existence.

My consciousness is completely unchanged and much clearer than in my normal state of mind, in which many external circumstances distract and influence me. This state of mind lasts for hours and cannot be defined in time and space. My first trip of this kind felt like I had not been in my body for weeks and spent weeks working on it, giving me insights into my thoughts that I'd never seen before. By that, I do not mean that I had flashbacks or did not get along with life. No, just the opposite but it took weeks to process all these insights and integrate them into my life.

These types of experiences change you. Whether through psychedelics, rituals or in other natural ways, experiences of this kind will always change a soul and with it the view of what you once called its box.

What does all this have to do with death now? I say everything. For many years, I have had many experiences that have personally demonstrated to me that although my body and my consciousness form a unity, my consciousness definitely gets by without a body. The way it looks the other way around, I cannot judge and only make assumptions, as I have never been in a state in which I have felt that my consciousness is completely disconnected and I am only my body.

The realization of this state, through many experiences and later the deliberate initiation of such states and the exploration of them, has changed and shaped my belief image so persistently that I am fully convinced that my consciousness is not related to the death of my body. If and how my consciousness can die and what exactly happens to consciousness is another theory. But then, it`s only one theory and possibly influenced by thoughts and theories of other people.

To what extent my consciousness can later interact with the external world is completely unclear to me. But I can imagine that if I only represent and am only aware of myself, I will probably recognize it in a box and try to climb over that edge again. Whether this border is another dimension, a kind of rebirth or interaction with this known world is not for me to the question. Because I will explore this box when the time comes and then find out in how far the limits are within our consciousness when I would live completely free in it and travel around.

Somewhereinmymind

In almost all texts that are in my art, I speak of this place as the name suggests, as somewhere in my mind. Whether it really is a place I can't say, definitely not in worldly reality. I would describe it as a state of mind. But for the sake of simplicity, I call it the secular word 'place', a place where my consciousness is completely free, a place where I like to escape and exist differently. I am fully aware of the worldly planet and with it all my memories and experiences that are related to it in my consciousness and, above all, my subconscious.

To describe this place is completely impossible for me, or to call this place 'place' is already too much a worldly term to describe what somewhereinmymind represents.

It comes very close to the state or a form of thoughtlessness. But thoughtlessness sounds a bit silly if you take it directly. So I rather mean the thoughtlessness in the sense of worldly biased ideas, of thoughts that are not based on free knowledge and therefore affect and influence my reality.

"My thoughts are free". A beautiful sentence but unfortunately completely wrong in its sense, I think because our thoughts are thoroughly biased. They are much too preloaded and thus these are anything but free and for me, every state of my mind in which this thought is included somewhere is the opposite of free. My subconscious mind is virtually the prison of my self since there are just those restrained thoughts that usually keep me from the kind of thoughtlessness that I mean when I speak of my place.

The place probably comes next to what I call freedom, or at least what I call deep inside of me as a perfect state of freedom. Free to look at something and interact unencumbered with it.

It's the place where I find the most inspiration for my art and my life.

Even though the word somewhereinmymind and most of my texts and things in my art deal with it, so far I have rarely talked about this place. Apart from that, I can't put this place into worldly understandable words.

In an open discussion, I was once asked if I create a world for myself with my art in which I can hide from the real world, or if my art is an extract from a surreal world in which I live mentally.

For many years, this has been a question about myself that I could not answer for myself or any other person.

By answering, I mean to give myself a completely conscious answer and to have an understanding of it myself, but not to philosophize or discuss.

At first glance, it is part of both. But that's like the question of the egg. What was there first the hen or the egg? One belongs to the other and perhaps there is no simple answer to this question. I also cannot understand how far what has arisen first. Since my art is definitely and mostly inspired by somewhereinmymind, it's still part of the creation that created it. Although I'm not sure if you create such a place yourself or if such a place already exists in each one of us, and you only have to find it in the depths of yourself. But even then it can be argued about whether the walls were already painted or I painted them afterward. As I said, I did not find a real answer to this question for several years, even though I have often thought about it.

But how important is it to find a perfect answer to everything? Not too important, I would say. Some things we should possibly just accept as they are and not let them distract us from real life.

Whether and how I have created this place and

created my life and my art, or whether all my absurd thinking about the worldly image, this place has created and has given me the greatest enrichment in my life, is not the question. It will also have no influence on what I refer to and will neither change my external nor internal reality with it. Both feed each other and grow into what I call life.

Somehow it's funny and absurd to write or talk about something that does not exist anyway, at least not in our outer real world. For most of my life, I am deeply affected by this place or feeling, no matter what we call it. It influences me deeply in my actions and life, especially in my creativity. It may also be important to have such an escape when confronted almost daily with things that rob you of all positivity and inspiration in your normal social life. And here I also speak of myself. It is very difficult for me to leave my little worlds and go out into the 'real' world, no matter where.

When I travel to beautiful countries, I am confronted with what the regular tourist does and how locals, anywhere in the world, simply rape beautiful places.

Or just to go to a psychedelic festival as someone who really loves psychedelic art, music, and that lifestyle, that has given his life for it and I promise you: It just hurts. I have had years of my life where I could hardly go anywhere anymore and left pretty soon, bringing me to the point where I created somewhereinmymind.

Knowing that I have a place that is completely protected from the whole gives me tremendous power

and motivation to confront myself from time to
time with more social situations.

Another point is that I create more small worlds
that I travel within next to Psyland. The easiest
way to do that in Europe is to simply turn our small
motorhome into a bubble of our own and, no matter
where I am, I have my little escape world with me.
But this, too, is just an excerpt from what I carry
deep inside me. Still a good feeling to know that
I just adapt the outer reality accordingly to feel
a little better in it.

When I started to give exhibitions and then one or
the other times too many people appeared for the
vernissage, I quickly hid in a street to avoid being
confronted. Which in turn is very silly when you
consider that you are actually doing exhibitions,
so you can allow others to gain more access to the
art I'm doing.

Maybe it was also the unfounded fear that it would
give more people access to somewhereinmymind. It's
hard to say and some things are only understood
in hindsight. Maybe I also had to realize that no
matter what I or others in the outside world do, it
doesn't have much impact on my inner world.

Most of those who know me personally know that I
have never really divulged much of what I created
artistically. Of course, I belong to the MySpace /
Facebook generation and thus had the opportunity
to show my creative work quite simply to a lot of
people. But most of the time I did not share more
than necessary or more or less used the whole thing
more for mischief, as I realized very quickly that
the whole social media world is not really what
you can do and create, but is much more about how

you market yourself. It was and is not the best thing for me, or rather, I put my time, motivation and heart into what I thought was more important and I always thought I let my actions speak for themselves.

Even today I still think that the most important thing for a person who wants to develop himself and who wants to find his own way is to break away from all thinking about his own reputation and status, whether with art, music or other things. You have to get rid of your ego, but you have to be self-confident enough to truly take that step. In my opinion, it is best not to take yourself too seriously and just destroy your reputation. Because once you get to the bottom you do not have to worry about doing something that other people think of as bad, you have the uncanny freedom to do and try things that are out of the norm.

When looking at myself for what I did as a tattoo artist, or better to say what I did as an artist with skin as a medium, I can say with hindsight that when I completely turned my back on the whole of my development, gave up on being a 'good' tattoo artist, gave up seeing myself as a tattoo artist, closed my studio and retired, and didn't go to conventions or other events and had phases where I had virtually no more publications and sometimes even gave no interviews for years, those were the years where I integrated more and more somewhereinmymind into my reality. The years in which my place of creation has also been transformed into something very absurd in what many in the 'professional' world of tattooing no longer considered professional. But why should I care, I was no longer a tattoo artist. But this gave me the freedom to create a space and a place

143

where the feeling is above everything. And that very feeling is what guides me and what is the origin of my creative work.

Most of those who came and come to me/us very quickly fall into this world. Many describe it as an escape from the real world and that's what allowed me over many years to work differently with the skin medium than other tattoo artists do. For the medium of skin is now more than another inner world and is far more personal than what touches the service of a tattoo artist. And to find this access, I opened my bubble and gave those who were willing to take a little step into somewhereinmymind.

If you want to touch the soul of someone you must not be afraid to touch his skin.

By that I mean I am not afraid of being blessed by someone I guide through a ritual or a period of life. Including all the sweat, smell and tears as all that belong to it.

My heart and feelings tell me if and how far I'm willing to lead someone through something like that. I think it is no secret that such an encounter with me is almost always associated with a lot of pain and crossing some other borders. And that requires a much more private atmosphere and mood, a private feeling if we want to call it that. And the most private thing I can reveal about my soul is a little insight into my own little world.

Now the most important part of this place, feeling or state, is probably that I carry this place in me at any time, deep in the world of my consciousness, deep in the world of my existence. And in the moments in which I travel my consciousness, it is now very easy for me to go to somewhereinmymind.

However, I fully understand that this place is not a real place viewed in terms of the external world. It is rather a state of feeling, a state of mind, or something in between which in return leads me, regardless of my outer shell, and makes it possible to visit this place. Also, I speak of states, no, especially in states where I have little or no control over my outer shell.

In which I drop my outer shell and leave my body.

Yes, especially in the states of mind where I completely detach from my human body. Whether through psychedelics or other rituals that allow me to initiate a state of my consciousness in which I can detach from my body and travel to my little escape world.

And now we come back to our actual topic. Because my digression on this subject has a great deal to do with death and has shaped and reshaped my idea of it very much. Because logically, from my point of view, I will have access to this place, no matter if and how far I am still connected to my body, and slowly but surely we get closer to the subject of death because this place and also the state of my mind in this regard has nothing to do with the earthly concepts like life and death.

The death

What is it that we understand by death?

I myself find the term "dying" very inappropriate because my idea of "what happens to my consciousness when I detach myself from my human shell" has nothing to do with what I've learned from the term "to die".

For me, death is no more or less than another form of consciousness, another form of existence, a next step.

Especially during my younger years, I had read and heard many views about life and death. Most of these ideas, however, I found very absurd and rather ridiculous, just a lot of religious ideas about what happens after death. Whereby death is always used to generate fear and implemented as a weapon to keep its followers in a certain religion.

Well, there will never be a real answer to this question. But if we are honest there is no perfect answer to any question in this world and our own faith is what should guide us, whether in life or after.

Should one see death as a threat? Should one be guided by death through one's life?

How far can I be able to accept what I don't know?

For me personally, death itself no longer poses any threat. Or death in the form of the dying of the human body does not scare me in any way. On the contrary, I now look forward to the experience that I will make one day. And that's exactly where we come to the big dilemma of the whole thing. What many people I have talked to about it and especially friends, with very different feelings left behind.

How far are death and life connected and are we aware of it? How far does one influence your life? How far can one influence his death?

I strongly believe that I can make the most of my life's conscious decision to die. By that, I do not mean that I like it when people kill themselves because they do not know how to continue or for other reasons want to end their lives, using it as the only and sole way to run away from life. Although I have to say here, that I find nothing wrong with it when people kill themselves for whatever reason.

The human survival instinct is very strong, natural and pronounced and therefore such a decision is always somehow considered and weighed. For some, living in this area may not be enough to hold onto as others do. Or maybe they just have more courage to finish the whole thing earlier than somehow necessary. Looking at it the other way, how many people are there who really don't feel like living and would rather be dead but just don't have the courage, the willpower or whatever it takes to leave their human life behind?

Suicide is unfortunately very contemptuously implanted in our society. In my opinion, this is definitely the last resort, but I think either way that will be the case with almost every individual who takes this step because to end your life you have to deal with it a bit.

So I am talking about a purely conscious decision for life. It's about the biggest amount of control you have over your life on this earth, the biggest decision you can make inside your outer human shell, the biggest decision of your life. Death is a very inappropriate term and also with everything that is not really what it represents for me.

For many years, during which I have created my new self-image to what we call death through a wide variety of experiences and experiences, the urge, or rather freedom, of one day has become more and more in control of me to make that decision. Not only to have this greatest aspect of life in your own hands but also because of other external and internal circumstances.

As our body ages and thus decreases in physical ability more and more, our minds grow and prosper. So it is in the normal human aging process and not when mental illnesses come along. Or, even then it is difficult to say how far people live consciously in their existence. Eventually, only pure physical communication with the external world will be very difficult or even impossible and will, therefore, be labeled as a pure mental illness by us. How many of these people think about throwing off their bodies and the burden of daily life? We can only guess, but I do not imagine anything worse than being trapped in such a body, to be kept alive by the family and doctors. Whether you like it or not, you have already lost a real influence on it.

I cannot imagine anything worse than the ability to lose control of my life and my death.

When we grow up as children and are not capable of many abilities and activities, it is mostly because our minds are not as ready as our bodies. But the older we get, the more we lose more and more skills. But now it is our body that continues to hold us back. The question is how far do we want to limit our consciousness in its abilities just because we cling tightly to our human shell. Why is it so hard for so many people to let go? Or why is it so difficult for relatives and friends to let go in some situations?

►► THE TRUTH ◄◄

THE BELIEVE WHAT MAKES PEOPLE
EASY TO CONTROLL AND GUIDE.

POWER··

RELIGION IS NOT TRUE AND REAL

> ONE HAS TO BE TRUE
> AND THAN THE OTHER
> WILL BE WRONG.
> GOD DIDNT MADE THE EARTH

SCIENCE ── (V.S.) ── RELIGION
            ═══

↑ SHIT
SCIENCE IS JUST BULL
WHO MADE THE EARTH
WHEN THERE IS A GOD

SCIENCE IS NOT TRUE AND REAL

TRUTH IS WHAT YOU BELIEVE
TRUTH IS BULLSHIT
AS MUCH AS IT IS GOD, SCIENCE
OR ANY OTHER BELIEVE SYSTEM
CREATED BY HUMANS

ONCE SCIENCE
PROVE THAT GOD
NOT EXIST.
THIS WAS WHY
THE CHURCH FIGHT
SCIENCE. ONCE GOD
WAS A EASY WAY
TO MAKE PEOPLE
BELIEVE. NOW
ITS SCIENCE.
WHAT WILL
COME NEXT.
WHAT COMES AND
PROVE, SCIENC
WRONG. ONCE
PEOPLE STOP
BELLEUVING IN
IT. NOTHING IS
REAL IS NOT
SOMETHING HOW
YOU CAN MAKE
PEOPLE FOLLOW
YOUR PATH !!!

WE MAY
THINK ITS CONTROVERSE
BUT IT ISNT. ITS PRITY MUCH
THE SAME SHIT.

Only the idea that old people say they want to end their lives is already so negatively solidified in our world view that it is almost impossible to kill oneself without causing guilt. Also, especially the idea that it is harder for the family or friends when you have killed yourself than if you died a natural death. I think that's why most people live so much longer than they wanted to and have an emotional dependency on acquaintances and family who hold them captive in something they might have wanted to let go of for a long time.

How many old people talk about death and say that they want it to be over?

Many family members might care about them and their wishes, but instead, they keep them alive and convince them to continue. Is it discussed in such families about how to die, for example? Can someone help his old mother if that's what she wants? Then families sit together and discuss such situations. Discuss the advantages and disadvantages. Talk about their mother's wishes and put them into their own? Or is it simply just this very serious and probably very well-considered statement suppressed in the wishful thinking that everything is so wonderful, so instead they are meeting for Christmas or a birthday and playing a great family, instead of actually giving a shit inside about how the other one really and truly is and what she or he wants.

The whole thing is so sick in my eyes and unimaginable. I'll talk more about that later.

How many old people now live longer than they want, just for exactly these reasons? Is this beautiful that you can live longer or just sad that they are kept almost against their will in their bodies? But if you never had your life completely in your hands, how should you have your death completely in your hands? Is it your fault or is it the problem of a society that tells us exactly what is right and wrong and can't accept a person's wish to end its own life?

Suppose our minds continue to travel with full consciousness, taking all that we have experienced with them in this dimension. How do we want to remember the last moments? As months or even years of torment or rather as moments of love where we see and feel that one's family and friends are totally there for us, no matter how and what we choose, no matter what our ideas.

What if the last encounters with friends and people we love is a small or minor dispute, with my partner, or an unimportant conversation with my daughter? Should that be the last thing that happens between us, the last words to remember later? Not holding it in the hand is a terrible idea for me that I could never make friends with.

How nice is the idea that with those you really care for, you can look him or her in the eye and tell them how much you enjoyed your time with them? These last words are deliberate choices and they can say goodbye properly and honestly. But such a circumstance is only possible in very few moments and if one clings too badly to the normal idea of dying, it is even impossible. In many normal social terms, even if you are already dying, it would be impossible to accept death and not fight it, and that you can say goodbye to everyone and everything.

To cling to life until one's death unexpectedly rips you out and robs you of everything you've always believed in, of everything we humans build on this earth, everything worldly. Unfortunately, that's what we associate with the word death and how likely most people are to leave their bodies.

For me, it is beyond question which option to choose. It is no longer a real choice if you are aware of this, purely objectively considered and discussed.

Also, the place and the event is in my hands, winter or summer, a period in which it feels worldly nicer to go, a place where you feel comfortable in the setting. If this becomes my ultimate experience of life, how far can I influence it to really and completely experience what I imagine to be the last journey out of my body?

How exactly I will solve these issues one day is something I don't know yet and I've not planned yet except for the fact that I want to be one of those who are pressing the 'button'. The last step is to walk across the border of death. I think it will take place in a way that on the one hand, no pain accompanies me, which in turn would sadden that experience. On the other hand, I think it would be nice if it does not mean to travel jerkily out of my body, but my human shell slowly ceases to function. Thus, I would be able to experience this journey and this border as consciously as possible.

Maybe it will explain to me the biggest mystery of life, or it will just be another small step forward, in the box that I call life. But this time it will not be a step I can share with any earthly soul. For if that were possible, that question would not be in the room, and death might not be a scary thing to most people.

Now let's go on and think about how many dreams and visions we have within us. Things or inquiries we always wanted to do. I am firmly convinced that we are dedicated to the realization of death, more to life than we will ever do under normal circumstances. If every day can be the last and we are aware of it, we will not postpone things until the next day, but rather use every option that is put before our feet. After all, who wants to lie on his deathbed one day and think about how many opportunities he has left unused, how many things he wanted to experience, and which he ultimately only pushed to the next day every day.

How far is it possible for us to influence our lives by accepting death for what it can be if we aren't afraid to die, or rather, aren't in fear of what awaits us after living in our human body. And here I'm talking about pretty much every idea of what can be. Everything is possible and everything can be beautiful. And this statement is not less realistic than that after that, nothing is more or the 'hell', where I personally can't imagine that you will be guided after death into something you don't believe in yourself. And why should I believe in things that are not completely positive? If I am so limited in the worldly envelope, then it will take even more time to believe that I will travel to something much more wonderful afterward.

Then we are no longer afraid of what awaits us after living on this earth. How far are fear and faith used to keep people in this template? It's an unfounded fear, but a fear that leads more people than anything else in the world. The Death.

The countdown of life

Based upon my own manifestation and belief in the perfect freedom to one day to take death into my own hands, I have come to another conclusion that has greatly enriched my life. Or rather, since I have made this conscious decision, it influences and inspires my life and especially my consciousness more than most of the other trains of thought that I have cherished in the past.

From the pure thought that one day it completely consciously separates itself from its human shell, I have moved on in thought over the years. Or better said, I was more driven by my thoughts. We live in this world with so much ignorance and lack of clarity that I have stopped searching for truth for a long time. Yet, I think it is possible for me in the area of my human body to live out certain freedoms and ignorance. In this context, it finally bothered me a little not knowing when the day of my onward journey is pending. Not knowing how much time I have left for the things I still want to discover whereupon it is not too absurd to take the whole somehow controlled and conscious realm into my own hands.

Wouldn't it be a wonderful idea to know when this day comes? Yes, even to determine when its day will come. How far is it possible to detach ourselves from the manipulated basic thoughts already within us and to see this decision as it really is and to judge objectively about this decision that I personally made. Free of whether you can personally identify with it or not. I am well aware that the decision about my death, for many people, and especially people in my immediate environment, represents a very frightening idea. Just as it has been very hard for me for a long time to talk about it and to people who are close to me and to communicate my vision of it.

I am well aware that all of this is related to our societally rooted ideas and therefore, no one of them is guilty of it. Because they are just as well as their parents and their grandparents outfitted and educated just to look at the world and its inhabitants as you should. Which in turn means that everything that goes far beyond this guideline is very difficult to view objectively.

At least for the first time and that's how most of them reacted, and initially it was unimaginable and not comprehensible. But with a little time in between, it was a bit easier for some people to pick up on this topic and look more objectively at it.

For me, this is one of the most beautiful and life-giving decisions I have ever made and almost incomprehensible, how negative some people take this decision. I feel no negative emotions or fears behind this event or the fully conscious decision on the timing of my onward journey. On the contrary, I am convinced that when this day comes I'll spend it with all the people who are truly important to me.

When that day comes I'm curious about what it will personally answer one of the biggest questions of my life. This day will probably be something as beautiful as you have never experienced with the subject of death. At least that's my idea of what I and the few people I'll have with me will experience and feel, without fear and regret in my eyes, without even thinking that I've not tasted my earthly life in the most perfect way.

Experience how a person breaks away from the earthly, consciously. Then this day will be remembered with joy and will enrich not only me personally, but I am convinced that it will call out to the people around me, my family and friends, the same emotional feelings as for me. It's not supposed to be the day I died, not at all, but rather, the day I lived more than any other day.

I am aware that for many people this idea is absurd or unrealistic but from what point of view? From a free-objective point of view, based on experience, or solely from the point of view of how we were raised from an early age and how death and dying were used as fear tactics and continue to be fed to us daily in various ways such as how suicide is interpreted in a way that one doesn't get along with life and is unhappy.

But an experience outside of the box as we know it, will indelibly manifest in our thought and then shape our world view to a degree that I'm convinced that, for example, my daughter is less sad so that she knows I am no longer trapped in the external world and have traveled on with full consciousness and that she always carries within me as before. That I lived completely free in this decision and was not simply torn from my life.

Especially when younger people leave, it is sad for most of them that they say something like, they still had so much in his life, so many dreams and goals, so many things they wanted to experience, etc. We all know what I mean. And that's definitely understandable, but somehow not, because most people put their real-life behind everything anyway and then stand in later years, looking back and the bottom line is that they did not realize much of what they wanted to do.

Life and death. It all depends on everything together and while many first work 60 years to attain a minimum of fulfillment from their lives, some people start very early and therefore inside feel to be a different age than what is written on paper.

How far my imagination is alienating me from what we call suicide, and whether and how to name it, is set. I'm sure the normal person will just say that I'm planning to kill myself, but that thought is so far from what is behind it in my head that I can't grasp exactly how to describe it in secular words because these, in turn, trigger different emotions in people, which are nothing more than already biased thoughts anyway.

And of course, I plan to kill myself, but at least I can somehow explain it logically and thoughtfully, while many exist in ways that are not much different from working to kill themselves. Take a smoker. They would probably deny it, but basically, it's nothing more than killing yourself every day or at least working on it every day. How should something like that not be planned? Just like alcohol or other drugs but yet society sees it differently and then it must be different no matter how many people die each year from cigarettes or alcohol.

Maybe the normal social person doesn't plan the exact date of his death, but he usually works on it at least where it seems to be a very creeping painful death in my eyes to compare with years of torture in the dungeon. Also, how many people consume medication because their immune system is virtually gone or take a lifelong intake of hormones, because of every little thing medication to name but a few things. Also, mental illnesses such as work-related stress, burnout syndrome, social pressure to succeed, anxiety, panic attacks, fear of failure and much more of what life in our society brings, especially if you persistently try to be part of it and to insist on it.

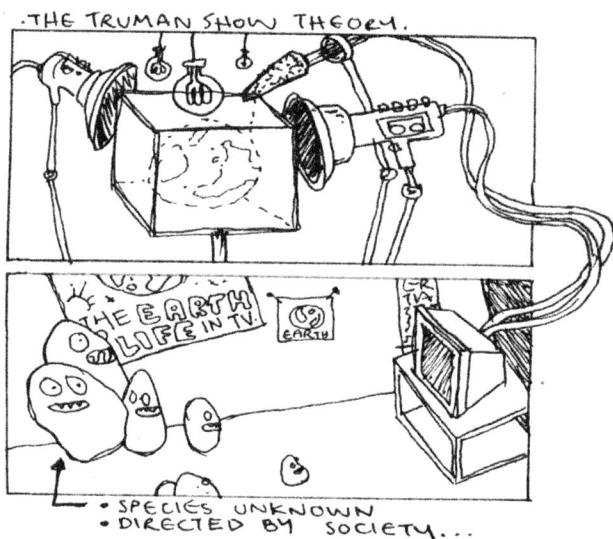

So when we look at it that way, it's nothing more than a long-anticipated suicide if you decide to lead such a life.

That's like the rape thing such as if someone is there and witnesses it but does not help. Then you are not just a cowardly human but you are also part of it. The moment you know what happens and know that you can change something with your actions, you are definitely responsible for what happens and

you (don`t) do and you cannot talk yourself
out of it.

So, if I know that my life does not make me feel unhappy, depressed, or otherwise as it should, then I seek a way out in legal or illegal drugs or substances, I try medication, hormones, therapies or whatever to convince me that my life is quite 'ok', at that moment I am well aware that I should actually change something and clinging to this life is nothing more than a long agonizing suicide. After all, I stand by mine.

So how do you calculate his lifetime?

Can you say that when you're 90 years old, you've lived more than someone who's only 60 years old? I know it is so well established in our society and it's good to be old regardless of what you experienced and how you used your time here.

So how do you calculate life and can tell if someone has grown old or not? Does one mean to become old, old in the form of life, or old only in the form of worldly years, no matter what one has done with his life at this time? Most would simply answer the question but I believe that many people, even at the age of 90, died very young in their lives in the way that I look at life as life.

If I already know that I am 47 years old, from a worldly perspective, does that mean that I die young?

If I have used these 47 years to fully live, 29 of them without wasting much time, then how much more of a full lifetime is that compared to many people who have left at the end of their lives?

Just a simple calculation, in Germany we have about 25-27 vacation days a year in a normal job, so if you plan something, with weekends and public holidays, you could make it into about 35-40 days in which you could leave your normal life behind and live completely free.

Assuming, of course, one works somewhere where one of these lengthy holidays would be approved in one piece, which is completely unrealistic for the vast majority of employees and many would receive at most 2-3 weeks holiday at a stretch. This is not too much time to travel, away from work to really get your head off work and to focus on what you want to do yourself.

If we count on 10 years to accumulate these stretches of vacation, it will give us about a year to focus on life. So, to live one year of a lifetime in 10 years in which you lead a normal social life does not just sound like a little, that IS little.

I became aware of this realization after making this calculation many years ago, whereupon I changed many things in my life. Because you can buy a lot of things, but time is not for sale. Time is my highest good. Time is my currency.

Time with my child, time to travel, time for things I wanted to do but with which I can't make money. While life tends to be about money most of the time, I have made time to strive for something worthwhile.

One day I made a similar calculation with sleep. If we sleep one hour less per day that adds 15 days a year. So with 2 hours less sleep per day, I have one month more waking hours of lifetime per year. After that, I trained my body to get along with significantly less sleep. Gaining one month a year more by sleeping for only 2 hours less? That's more than a good deal and most of the time it's more

than a few more hours that I pick out that I'd
rather fill with life.

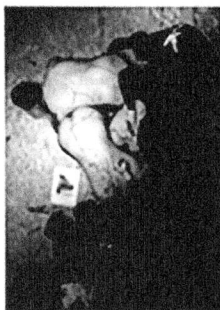

That does not mean that I do not like to sleep. I notice how my body needs sleep and I give it plenty of it. I am also not one who does not sleep at night, because that, in turn, obscures the consciousness. Only by myself did I begin to adapt and train my complete sleep rhythm more and more.

I am definitely a day person and I love light and sun. The human body also builds hormones over daylight to ensure deep sleep. Also, I have taught my body that I live with very little sleep and thus I get in the normal rest very quickly, in the deep sleep phase and REM sleep, which is actually the only recovering sleep.

Of course, by eliminating the other sleep phases, I naturally gave up a few other things in terms of sleep technology.

I have almost no dreams since then but whether it is because I skip the other sleep phases or just go down into my consciousness as far as possible in deep sleep, I can not say exactly. That probably depends on both, and if I wake up in the morning and do not get up, but then go on sleeping in a less deep phase, then I have normal dreams. And yes, dreams are fun and I like them too, but they still do not value giving me so much time. Apart from that, in my real life, I experience at least as many absurd things as I'd encounter in my dreams.

Is living a lot of life?

When I think that for 12 years, I lived in my time and have another 17 before me. That means for me, from the perspective of what I have already experienced and how my life has developed through this way of life that In otherworldly years I've probably experienced 100 times more than what I would have ever dreamed. The question is rather how I am to support my body over the years, more than too often beyond human limits. My mind will certainly not stop, that's relatively clear to me.

If you ask me if I want to grow old I would say "yes", although I am aware that this statement from the normal social point of view, is not nearly true from the perspective of the secular years.

But should I put this strange illustration above my own?

And yes, many wonder about what sense it makes to set this day so early, to set a countdown. Apart from the point that one is completely free to choose the season, the time and especially the place where one moves on one day, that aside to plan with whom to spend this last day or the last days. Apart from these not so small points, it's pure freedom.

How much life does death bring?

Imagine you are sitting with a doctor for a check-up and you are told that you have found a tumor and you still have 6 months to live. How do you think this statement will change your entire life? Not your life in the form of human existence at this moment, but your life in the form of life from that day x on.

I cannot imagine anyone out there, just going on these 6 months living as they had before. Unchanged as they'd lived before and then unexpectedly dying alone after 6 months. That is no longer possible because one expects death and one is confronted daily from day x onwards.

Such a fundamental confrontation with death breaks just about every one out of life. And in 6 months you can experience so much, maybe more than in a whole life, where you push every dream only to the next day. Once you get a countdown, there's no turning back. Only forward.

I personally believe that the positivity you carry from such a countdown is in no relation to what you give for it. To carry on such a countdown that always tells you how much time you have left. The one daily, hourly, even monthly reminder how much time you have left to live. Yes, exactly, such a countdown will not have any negative effect on your life.

When we no longer see death, but life, when we look at this clock and see that it is our life. That it's all the things we have to experience and do in our bodies on this earth. For me, it's not the countdown to death but the countdown to life.

We all carry this countdown in us.

Man is transient. Our life on this planet is transient.

But how far do we want to be ignorant and deny our own countdown? As macabre as it sounds to many, but I consciously carry my countdown externally because I am aware of my life and its transience in this external world.

Knowing when that day has come and knowing how I can and want to use my time before that brings me, in my opinion, a big step forward, a step further than I would be if death unexpectedly pulls me out of my present life. I still wanted to do some things but had no time for it. That's the way it is, but you have the time if you are just aware of it.

If you put ten things on a list that you want to put in your box before you die, but you know you only have time to experience 5 of those things then one will deliberately weigh which things are more important compared to the others. And even if you really want to, then you might also experience 6 of them, or if you do not sleep you can maybe do eight. Or you say that only one point of it really is fundamentally important and you want to savor it all the more. But to come to such a point of consideration and decision, many people have to first have an experience to become aware of their countdown.

17 years 78 days 7 hours 49 minutes

(My remaining lifetime at first version of the text)

SOCIETY GAME

Society

In my opinion, this is one of the greatest mysteries of our human existence, something that has shaped us more and continues to shape and guide us, as we love each other.

How far are we able to live our lives completely free as long as we live in society? Freedom. Whatever may hide behind this little word, I believe that we will never succeed in finding any approximate reference to it as long as we move within our Human Envelope, located deeply in what we call society.

The freedom of one stops where the freedom of the next begins. But does true freedom have some sort of boundary and end? Probably not. And in the already overpopulated world we are living in, there seems to be some risk involved if the individual person had too much free space for his or her own development. In that sense, we can imagine freedom as small packages and life itself as a Tetris game. Because where the fields are already full we cannot lay down a new part and so on. So this means to reschedule your freedom nice and bravely around the others. But somehow, first of all, that doesn't work out so peacefully and well, and second, even less do I see the people living in it in some sort of freedom.

Probably coexistence would no longer be possible in this way even though we can't talk about a peaceful coexistence in relation to the human being anyway. Because otherwise I cannot explain wars and murders and all that happens here on this earth.

What is life?

Once we are aware of our body and its transience,

aware of how far our lives and future lives are, and when we're more dependent on the reality of others than on our own, then it is more than time to change that.

I suspect that no matter how satisfied the majority of people are with their lives, or rather no matter how those people have their reality shaped to be content with the existing deep within every soul probably realizes that all this is just shit. Not everything society tells us through television and the media is true or that wars do nothing more than to serve the enrichment of a few or that the individual is probably less an individual than he is capable of being. I am convinced that even those who are deeply rooted in society and have achieved high social rankings have one or two doubts, probably those who are not even trying to fall asleep in the evening without being completely knocked out with sleeping pills or drugs.

And now here's maybe a very tough comparison. When we see three men starting to rape a little girl in a side street. Are we the kind of human who'd intervene even though we know that we could be beaten up enormously or even worse may end up happening to us? Are we willing to accept suffering to prevent this? Or are we cowards and call, if at all, only the police. Knowing that the damage would be irreparable until the cops arrive. Is it enough to convince yourself later that you have done everything in your power to help and you can fall asleep again with a clear conscience?

I myself am a pacifist throughout. Although this does not mean anything in such a situation and you can still intervene or have to, if you know yourself otherwise you can't live later with the uncertainty that you might even have warded off worse.

And to put it plainly: Just because I despise violence, it does not mean that I am a philanthropist. The human being is, in my opinion, the biggest culprit on this planet and if I had the chance to do something about it, I would use it.

In my opinion, most of the people live in a cowardly way, no matter in which context. I wish I could teach them better, but most of what I've experienced in my life just makes me sad. Even those who are dissatisfied and are aware of their lives or of at least some of the dissatisfaction contained within them rarely take action to intervene. The fear of consequences seems to slow most people down. For who wants to be bloody on the ground and have the society in superior power as an enemy?

I remember talking to my dad when I was about 20. He just didn't want to understand how I've gotten into situations that had complicated my life over and over again. And by that I mean complicating it from his point of view, or from a more normal social view. He wanted to explain to me that I could have a "good" life with what I do if I wouldn't always get stuck. What he told me is that there is a reason all fish swim with the current in a stream as they come much further that way than to fight against it.

I thought about it and I was aware that there were these fish, whereupon I told him that I am probably the one who also binds a board on my back so that the whole thing is not too "easy" as those who swim with the current never see the source and the origin of what they call their life. I'm probably still the one who makes a small challenge out of it, so it will not be too easy.

If I sit here now and look back, I really have to laugh. Since I know that this was probably a stupid yet funny answer then. But that probably describes exactly what and how I have led my life since then. And 11 years later, I'm sitting here and I know my life could have been so easy.

But a boring simple life without answers wouldn't have given me the struggles or answers. So I guess I'll unlock another board and move on. Only this time with the conscious knowledge that I will never find answers and even less an origin or a true meaning of life.

Stupid sayings like, "Life is what you make of it" are true. That's exactly the case! Everyone has the way in which he lives his life on earth. There are no excuses, no apologies and with the awareness of his countdown, there is no "leave if for later".

I would not even go so far as to say that only a certain layer of over privileged people are capable of doing so. Clearly, some may have easier conditions, and thus the start is much easier. But looking at the bottom line, we're all alike. Whether we are now growing up in the favelas of Caracas or on the beach of Miami with super rich parents. Every situation brings and holds its advantages and disadvantages.

Because it is what it is, it is our life in the "here and now". After my assumptions, here on this planet we have only one life and it would be a pity not to use that in the breadth and depth of our possibilities. Or rather we do not have every opportunity to lay ourselves down and do everything we can to use our lives as we really and completely want.

When I was young, I read a lot of ideas, Krishnamurti, Osho, and many more who questioned our society. Likewise, I had read various religious worldviews and, in contrast, scientific theories of the earth and of existence. Even though I later went on to read other ideas, it has opened my mind at this time very much and I kept in mind that there are as many worldviews as people and yet most in them are pre-programmed versions. Stuck.

Pre-programmed? When I grow up as a Christian, I am also set up to know that this is the truth and the existence and meaning of life. Compare this to a computer. If we had one at home and there was only one program on it, let's say a writing program and we're now growing up in a community where everyone has just that one program on their PC and no one ever heard of other features, then this is the reality for us and very few would question it. Then further questioning would begin and eventually reveal that there are far more possibilities than those we already know or know.

And if not, then it would lead to simply creating new opportunities, meaning new programs. And suddenly we would be able to use the full potential of the computer and have access to thousands of programs. But as long as we cling to it or accept that there is only one usage function, we will never know what is really possible.

If science is only one program, and religion is

another, then this book is just a tiny little self-written program.

Many of my roots are, as before, in all sorts of different subcultures, which I have been on the verge of experiencing and exploring in my childhood. But really, I really never wanted to be part of a subculture or a sub-society. This non-adaptation expresses one very quickly to the margins of society, or to the very edge of any other form of society, subculture or grouping.

From this I realized early on that society, and with it, all its pre-programmed thoughts and values, will never allow me a safe life.

But what exactly is society and what is it trying to do?

One thing is clear to me, when so many people live and act together; there have to be rules and norms. It is even simpler, of course, similar to genetically manipulated fruit, which is bred and changed directly into the appropriate form, to do something similar in humans. It is quite easier to manipulate someone from an early age so that he later lives with his own values as he should in the eye of society rather than one day ban or take things away from him. That in turn would have tremendous consequences, since humans would then become aware of their own cage. The person would be robbed of his liberty essentially and clearly the consequences might be an acute rebellion.

Of course, our society, and with it those who govern it, always strive to be one step ahead. There are of course many ideas, which I will not go into here now, but amusingly, I have some sketches and drawings distributed in the book. None of that matters, but none of that, in my view, is more unrealistic than what we are sold as "the truth".

Personally, I have pretty much discarded any idea or belief of what might be, as it would not affect my life either way. I loved all those conspiracy theories, illuminati, sub-societies, higher powers, and everything that is behind it.

But even if someone convinced me 100% of the truth of an idea, it would still be meaningless and not impact how I live and what my own reality is. When I once abandon the idea of a perfect truth or idea, it does not immediately mean that nothing is possible, but that everything is possible.

The moment I believe that the earth is round I reject any other idea. But the moment I reject this idea, I create the space and the possibility that everything is possible.

I have met a few people in my life who've said; if you do not believe in anything completely and therefore nothing is important, it must be incredibly difficult.

But it is not that much harder to believe in something that is most likely not genuine. And there I find the example of the round earth very nice. There are definitely facts and examples that clearly show that the Earth is not as it is shown to us through the mouthpiece of science. And just because we're shown a photo or society tells us it's so, does not mean it is reality. Well, it's not that difficult to believe it. Especially when you confront yourself with the opposite.

How is it possible for the sun to shine through the clouds at angles that would never be likely if it were actually so much bigger than Earth and so far away? How is it possible that when we look out to sea, we see no rounding or curvature in the horizon? Again, I do not want to go into more detail because for me, any theory is equally realistic and unrealistic. I just want to suggest that in my opinion it seems much harder to cling to something and believe this while anything can be possible.

For a long time I searched for answers until I came to the point where I just let go of it. It's hard to say if it's the fact that I would not fully accept an answer anyway, or that no answer would change anything in my own life. But as long as one adheres to answers and needs them to lead one's life, it seems difficult to understand how easy it is to live without faith.

And suddenly everything is possible.

Society game

That is one of my very early tattoos and one of the few that I still wear visibly on my thumb because in the whole it's just that for me.

Society plays with us in every way. But who tells us that even small-targeted rebellions, subcultures, conspiracy theories and so on, are not part of this game? Meant to confuse us. Part of throwing us a piece of freedom and giving us questions we are supposed to ask. Questions that have no bearing on what really happens to us humans and probably just distract us from the real issues.

In this regard, so many things happen in the media that just testify. If most people go to a demonstration or the like, they may really think they are making a difference and showing it to the state. But how far is this questioned? The venues and times are usually determined by the state to completely control the subsequent reaction. And most of the protestors, who cause damage at such a demonstration, damaging houses, cars, shops, etc. from other private individuals, think that they really did make a difference and the state itself does not do any harm.

It is probably like a forest fire in which you deliberately set up a counter fire to stop the actual fire.

Pressure relief valve. Just saying.

Because, by throwing a piece to the "simple human ", he can react, you prevent that something from really getting started and then exploding in a frame where it's too late to intervene. Uncontrollable behavior.

Let's assume that instead of 2-3 pointless demonstrations a year, everyone involved would come together and burn down the town halls in one big city every day. It's unthinkable what would happen then in a country. Perhaps if everyone burned down all the central main banks, then what impact would it have? The bottom line is that they cannot change, or possibly only very few are willing to really want to change something.

Or the simple man is really that stupid that he really and truly does not see it and really depends on the threads of society as I suspect. For many years I am constantly confronted with it and I just do not want to believe that in this context man is really so stupid and blind. Unfortunately, almost every day I am taught better. In fact, it's not even his own fault, because he too is just a habit-bull, educated just as much by people who have been educated in the same herd mentality and so on and on and on.

For the greatest goal of society is and always will be that the simple human being does not think about his own existence and continues to follow what he thinks is right.

Yes, I too am a part of the society.

For a long time, I saw it that way and claimed that it is not possible to live freely outside of our society. When I was younger, I thought I was living somewhere out of the way, or at least I could live outside of society. But the longer I study all of this, the longer I am part of and live in it, and the more I become aware of it. How far we humans are held in it. Any kind of person, no matter how free and easy he or she seems to live.

Yes, I see myself as part of society, even though I am aware of where my place is in it. For myself, I seek this place as far as it is possible for me to live in this external world. I'm not a philanthropist and probably never will be. I am not a hippie or a philosopher, teacher or anything of this kind trying to change the world trying to help people. I try to take as little from society as possible and give it as little as possible. Everything that is in the range of my possibilities and ideas, let's call this the edge of the social gray area, this is my place where I built my little world and where I try to live.

Even if it sounds stupid, the only teacher is you. The only shaman is you. The only god is you.

Understanding this brings you further than anything else. Because anyone who wants to lead and influence you in one form will also change you in some way, a way that may go away from your own. Does this mean that you have less experience without a teacher figure or external influence? Or is it possible to assume that exactly this experience is not a free experience and accordingly cannot really contribute to creating one's own reality? I personally put the learning from my own experience of any experience that is transmitted to me almost second-hand.

Which does not mean that one can't exchange their ideas, learn anything, or listen to and read any other's worldviews. No, but one can understand that these are the ideas and life of other people. Just as this book is nothing more than my view of life and is not intended in any way to mentally manipulate or influence anyone. It's just another gibberish of human words about a little soul trapped inside, meaningful enough for myself to spend time writing, but also somehow completely insignificant for tomorrow.

And only by approaching something consciously and purposefully can you develop yourself further. This can make you ask questions; questions for yourself that only one person can find answers to. And that is you yourself. Because the moment you go with your questions to a teacher, god, shaman or anyone else will you get his answers? Answers that can be as different as diverse as humans and their ways of life.

I do not necessarily mean that it is absolutely correct to completely discard any kind of external information and to give them no value. Depending on the situation, other opinions can also help you to doubt your own already created views and to question them again. Which may create another new opinion image.

I myself am a very interested person of what is happening around me and I suck all information on what is somehow interesting. However, at the same level, I am a very ignorant and intolerant person in relation to outside information that is not based solely on my own experience and 'free knowledge'. I would not necessarily consider this property as something bad, but simply as my personal precaution to protect myself from external influences.

Go with the same problem to a doctor, to a shaman, to a crazy faithful pastor and then to a miracle healer. And now compare all the answers, advice and healing measures with each other. It quickly becomes clear to you how different these are and that it is actually not possible for all of them to represent their own truth.

Whether and how far any of their ideas can help you is always entirely up to you. If I really believe in it, then a doctor will help you as much as a healer or a guru. But the moment I cling too much to something and look at that vision as ultimate truth, I also take the opportunity to enrich my life with other ideas.

It is sometimes difficult for me to put this into words, because I don't really believe in anything, but I am open to everything, which, however, I then totally doubt in its reality, authenticity or mode of action. In the end, I don't believe anything that I haven't experienced myself, but in a way also doubt my own experiences as long as they're based on externally experienced circumstances.

Of course you can try to accept a strange truth, but to what extent it will bring you forward in your own personality is very doubtful.

Well, for many years it has almost become a hobby of mine to study "normal society people", if you like to call it that. The little time I have to go to a city or a place where I am confronted with many people is very seldom, just enough to sit on the edge of the street or watch people in front of a café, watch fashion and trends, and observe normal human behavior and its templates. It is omnipresent. And I speak of any kind of society, subcultures and subgroups, which I'll explain in more detail later.

Why do people like it so much to adapt and insert in such a way?

That's a question I've been carrying around for many years and just do not understand. Or. Cannot answer. Of course I can probably answer it but I just don't care to understand it.

The normal man is probably a lazy animal, which is rather blind led and directed. Where there are no questions you don't have to search for answers. So most take everything that is sold to them as reality. And the longer one is in the social control apparatus, the harder it will be to put it off. And that starts in early childhood and our parents have been programmed so far that they do nothing more than to direct this in turn to their own children in order to let them vegetate in the same way in the world as they have always done themselves.

What are trends and fashion and why does everyone really want to look the same?

Is it a way to hide and thus adjust its shell? Are not many of them even aware of how to get themselves uniformed, or is it a form of distraction to distract the simple human from things and things that really happen around him? No matter what it is, it seems to work. The average person works hard to spend his money on things he probably does not even like. But no one has said that being part of a society is easy.

But now I just talk about the outer shell, in which each person shows himself to the world, and on the inside, it is even more adapted, I think.

Our society is not stupid and if everyone was wearing a uniform then that would be way too obvious. Where there are still countries and cultures today where there is something like a uniform. Let's think of the burkas and full-body veiling. Most people in the Western world shake their heads, but on the other hand, they do not dissociate themselves very much.

The burka of the western world is just called fashion.

This in turn changes over and over again to present the normal person something like a refreshing novelty. I refer to it as a modern ignorance and actually, through fashion, and the compulsion it brings with it, people rob more individuality than they actually know.

One is convinced by television and media, advertising and prominent personalities, of what one likes and what one currently wants or even must have. Most of the time these things seem to be so good, then suddenly not so great when the next fashion enriches the market.

We can, for example, compare with colors. Then you could say that many are busy trying to find out who has the best, the craziest, the most outrageous, the most outrageous green, completely ignoring the fact that everyone is running around in "green" and other colors still exist. Until one day the whole thing is maxed out so that the system has to update itself so that the normal person does not notice the green abundance. And then miraculously, something like 'red' is initiated, before it attracts attention, and most likely it will paint and attract everything 'colorful'. And colorful is not a color and will not be tolerated. Perhaps it is a stupid comparison but sometimes it feels like that when I watch people for an hour in a city it is a completely colorless spectacle of modern uniformity.

In my most extreme time, before age 20, I'd always turned my t-shirts inside out before putting them on as my own small silent protest against the media-influenced homogeneousness that we humans go through.

Our society is updating.

More and more things are finding acceptance that were once unimaginable. But is this really freedom? Sure, when we look back at the generations before us, it certainly looks like we have a lot more freedom and quality of life these days than we used to. And that's probably what every generation will look like when they look back and even when they look ahead to the newer generation. How far is this really the acceptance for a life that is freer, if it's true reasons are connected with it to prevent exactly this?

Tattoos for example. In the past, tattoos were socially negative. Tattooed were outlaws, sailors, rockers and of course criminals. Tattoos were either hidden from society or shown proudly as a sign of abandoning the normal social life. I do not want to go into that, because I think we all know what I mean by that. Especially those of us who were already clearly visible tattooed before the age of Facebook and Instagram.

At the present time, it is already fully socially acceptable to be tattooed in the Western world, and one can even gain leadership positions with visible tattoos or piercings. In the meantime we find tattooed people everywhere and even in advertisements, media etc. they are taken to a company, e.g. to give a young, modern and open image. It is indispensable in our generation.

But to what extent does it really give us more freedom, or is it just another point to keep the normal person in the invisible cage? When I tattooed my fingers back then, it was still a big step, since at that time I had basically built my future on a good job and a good life. But that was exactly what I wanted and what I needed then. I wanted to destroy my normal social life and not to lose the thought that there would be a return. And that was a great deal of freedom for me at the time and purposeful to take a step like this and not because it was accepted or was cool. No. Just to let go of a normal future. I was well aware that it would be a different and heavier life but it was my decision with everything that came with it.

Nowadays, this step is very small. For one thing, the society now has significantly more 'tolerance' and, on the other hand, there are now great laser devices to undo such things. I could puke when people come and tell me how great it is that now everyone can live like this and it's so great that society accepts that. And again we are in modern uniformity, in our burka, so to speak. But very few people notice that at all while moving on in the illusion of freedom. For exactly this was taken with it and a great and possibly life-changing step was something completely meaningless.

Another point I always find interesting to address is social holidays or other occasions.

How far is the normal human being trapped in it? I specifically use the word "trapped". Let's take something like Christmas. Apart from the fact that it was once a purely Christian festival. Apart from that, Christmas is a very good example for what I like to talk to people about.

Why do we celebrate such festivals as Christmas anyway?

The answer is then how nice it is that the family meets and gives you something and so on but from what kind of view?

I find it very sad that it is not possible for many families to get together without social holidays or other occasions and spend a nice evening or a day together. And the year has 52 weeks apart from statutory holidays, so 52 weekends where the normal person does not work and has time to meet with his family. Likewise, there are holidays and if you really want and have a reason for yourself, then you would certainly easily find time for it. So

I cannot really take that as an argument, if any, as a very bad and unimaginative one.

Or just give something if you feel like it and think of someone. Because you might see something somewhere where you know it would be a good gift for a friend or family member as then this gift would come from a pure heart and just because you think of this person. It would be a perfectly casual gift and would have much more meaning. But most people need days like Christmas or birthdays to give a gift to others or the emotion of thinking about them.

But does one do that, or is it just the normality, or the compulsion that one must give something on such days? Does one then give out of free pure heart or out of a compulsion? How many run aimlessly through the city before Christmas or birthdays to find gifts for people to finally have something to give instead of standing there with empty hands?

Having nothing to offer would definitely be disappointing and hurtful. So you would rather give something, where you may not even know if that would be the best gift for the person.

But yes, the constraint binds the human being and it is not even questioned.

How sad is this whole game and somehow there is almost everyone in it. Personally, I have filed these days away very long ago. Especially if you have a child it is more difficult. As my daughter in turn is aware of such things, but knows that she receives from me, for example, a gift on her birthday or on other such days. If anything, it is a nice and appropriate gesture that you should perhaps give your parents or mother something for your own birthday. That would definitely make more sense and is in turn one of the little rituals I have given my daughter. Through my entire dealings with her, she understood early that I don't need special days to show her my love. To do something special with her or just to give her something, because I see it and think about how perfect the present would be for her.

This is the same with friends. Every gift I give comes from a pure heart and therefore has a very different meaning than a gift enforced for holidays.

And sure, if you like the tradition of having a solid day to meet as a family, why not create them yourself? Why not create an individual family day with your own tradition and your own ideas of when and how such a day would be? Then you would have complete influence on this day and I am aware that it would be something that would be more beautiful for most families than a forced day based on foreign traditions.

Our society.

We all live in it, but very few really do question it and question their captivity in the whole. Maybe we live in a cage bigger than our imagination. But does that mean that we are really free and that our actions are completely free? Or is this just another template that keeps us trapped in the whole thing?

Another topic that is a good example in our day and age is how society keeps us in its templates and throws us a bit of imaginary freedom like modern media and social platforms, the Internet and everything that goes with it. Here I am aware of the possibilities that such a thing as the Internet offers and how easy it is to connect with people we love. While I used to completely shun my cell phone or Internet while traveling, every few days I used the opportunity to stay in touch with my daughter via Skype, no matter where in the world I was. I am also well aware that much of my life on the platform today is based on the Internet and it gives me the opportunity to simply distribute my art throughout the world and thus live a freer and more independent life.

But how much should one lose oneself in this whole world? For many it is a kind of escape into another world, a world in which they are more important than they are in real life. How far that personal freedom goes is hard to say. But it's definitely some sort of outlet, allowing people to live their lives without having any direct impact on their outer lives. What a pity, but the people, again, have a bit of freedom thrown to their feet.

Especially when I'm traveling I notice it all the more clearly. Or let's say, the more I face people and walk past places where many ordinary people are. It seems to me that nowadays the simple mental memory of an event or an experience has apparently become little worthwhile. Everything is photographed and documented instead of experiencing the pure experience itself. Photos of themselves in the temple, in the sea, at meals, at concerts and so on, seem to be more important than to fully enjoy the moment. In a way it's nice to share your experiences and share them with friends and family. But how far is this documenting the moments a top priority when you can't even manage to turn this off and restrict it on vacation?

Especially where holidays are what many people don't have in excess and that once a year where the whole family flies away and wants to switch off for two or three weeks then you should actually enjoy it. But then I see entire families in the restaurant or on the beach, everyone with their smartphones in their hands and even young children who are already immersed in this illusory world. Whole families communicate with each other only through a screen.

It is also easier to build a phony world than to adapt to your own reality to the extent that you find more contentment in it.

How far are we dependent on such things? It has been a long time since I had this dependence on my mobile phone. At that time, I still had a normal tattoo and piercing shop and the need to be reachable. Yes, the normality to always be reachable. Every time I travelled and left my cell phone at home, I arrived back in Germany after one or two months and hated switching my phone back on.

Until I just came back one day from hiking alone in South America. I came back and looked at my phone. That was the moment when I just did not turn it on anymore. This is now about 7 years ago and I feel much better since I am no longer reachable.

Which does not mean that I avoid any use of it. I even have an emergency mobile phone, which I have from time to time in my backpack or in the car and which helped me in one or the other breakdown or situation very much. But I'm not reachable over it and I have filed the urge or the normality of being available.

Subcultures

I guess I belong to the generation that has seen some of the old subcultures on the sidelines. While I was young, I was already convinced that everything was already too late and destroyed. But now, several years later, I have to admit that it was nice to see something even more important than what subcultures became in the meantime.

The basic idea of every subculture is actually something beautiful as people who try to break out of their normal bourgeois life, who want to turn their backs on society. Eventually even the society wants to clarify how bad it is to the people and want to draw attention to the outside by appearance and behavior. I myself could never completely adapt and fit into a subculture. Even though I learned, read and experienced a lot about their different stories and backgrounds. As a result, it quickly became clear to me that even life in an extreme form, within a subculture, is nothing more than life in society.

Because, within each sub-society there are again new rules, laws and definitely very strong behavior patterns along with an almost more pronounced uniformity duty than compared to our normal society.

Because you want to belong and that goes way beyond simply being mentally on the same level and wanting to escape the fabric of society.

I have always hated the idea of adapting to anything and, as much as I approve of any idea and type of subculture, I am aware that it would never find a place in a life where I can live completely free.

Again and again I went into subcultures, and spent

a lot of time with friends who were represented in the most diverse fringe groups like Skateboarding, Punk, and Hardcore. In the early years I'd been oscillating between small Goa parties and punk concerts and it has given me much sustainability to realize that I've always seen my place in each of these groups on the sidelines and not as a part of it, between everything, but nowhere. As a silent observer, sitting silently on a floor somewhere to observe and study the whole spectacle. And whether I'm not fit for inclusion in normal society or subculture does not make too much difference to me.

If anything I've seen myself as a skateboarder. Which on the one hand was a beautiful subculture, on the other hand a lifestyle, which has later, like most things in our society, been updated and adapted through time. But I don't want to digress too long over how and why individual groups went to pieces. I just want to mention again that I'm glad to have gotten to know some of the roots and to see for myself how the society adapts to this.

Straight Edge - SXE

However, I would like to make a short statement about that, because it has become fashionable again today and does not have much in mind with its original meaning.

Once it was a sub-grouping that originated from the original Punk-Hardcore roots and still influences me very much in my life. Even if I do not see myself as part of it and have not really seen it as such. Ironically, I had several straight-edge tattoos and still carry a few signs of it today. Although my starting point was never that I had left society as part of this subculture, I found the idea beautiful, that tattoos were a very radical expression to emphasize this attitude once again. Especially the early SXE scene had Big X tattooed on their hands to avoid alcohol at concerts and other events. Since at that time all minors got big X painted on their hands to prevent them from getting alcoholic drinks. Of course, such tattoos were a big and lifelong statement.

Once upon a time, the more extreme subculture punk hardcore has realized how much alcohol and drugs are part of our society, and the most radical among them have stopped taking these things completely to step further out of society. To show that at concerts and in life you do not need excuses like alcohol or drugs to behave like an 'ass', living free and conscious and, above all, as the highest and most important point, against our society.

Like many others, this subculture is dead. Nowadays, it's just cool to be SXE and most of them live their normal social lives and forgo drugs, alcohol etc. for a variety of reasons. But the true essence of what it used to be is unfortunately forgotten, as in any other kind of subculture.

Maybe this is just nonsense and my perception just fades out all those who are not fully behind their attitudes and principles and then finally there is not much left. To be truly radical and to live by its principles is not a simple step, and more difficult than ever before due to our social updates.

I personally love radical people.

Still, I see myself as part of SXE, after which I tattooed "lsd-X-edge" on my arm and "psy-X-core" in my hand. As an indication that I have said goodbye to any kind of consciousness-limiting substances and that I still live like this for over 14 years. But over the years I've found more and more of psychedelic substances and their mind-expanding effects, this has only become more intense, and I have no need for any substance that robs me of the ability to be completely myself in my consciousness.

And there we are with a difficult to understand topic for the normal person, because he knows that, for example LSD is a very strong drug, which is clearly negatively charged. And of course it is illegal. While something like alcohol is socially tolerated and thus is indeed perfectly legitimate to consume. Well, things do not work that simple in my life. I do not want to go much deeper into this topic now either. Only so far that may be much of what we have been told is not quite true.

Yes, psy-edge or whatever you want to call it, because there is no suitable subculture for this type of form and probably and hopefully will never exist, because that in turn would only force people to categorize and adapt somewhere. The free form of life would flow again and somehow everyone has to find their own way.

Back to the subcultures. I like to use the words "social update" or "societygame". Because that's what society does to us. Subcultures especially are a beautiful example and I personally have followed them for many years as the society has updated in this regard. Let's take punks. Once they were a thorn in the eye of society and above all by their appearance, especially in public.

Say, if the normal person has seen a punk on the street, that in turn has raised questions in him and in turn inspired him to think. Why are such people so dissatisfied with society and life? And yes, the simple person should not think so. The simple man should follow and live in the illusion that he lives a beautiful life or that he has at least the opportunity to gain a beautiful free life if he just settles hard enough in society.

What is society doing to solve these problems? It's updating itself. Let's call it a relief valve to which I'll come back to later. This pressure relief valve is supposed to prevent the normal person from asking too many questions. So we feed him with something we call 'freedom'. With freedom he can be fed many possibilities. My theory behind the whole social update is that by some circumstances and influences, a kind of tolerance is created in our society. On the one hand, this tolerance conveys freedom within a certain marginal grouping or subculture, and at the same time it adapts the rest of society to the extent that it no longer feels disturbed by it. Say, no more questions.

The whole thing I had previously addressed with the topic of tattoos.

As another simple example, let's take the punks again. Once you have seen a punk to be determined by external characteristics, which in turn symbolized by his appearance, a certain attitude towards life and attitude to society, on the street and it has just triggered exactly what I have described. Questions have been raised, etc.

Now we'll take 'punk' and hurl it through the update. With the benefit of media, television, celebrities, etc., society is quickly making a trend out of it, and thus increasing its tolerance and thus the adaptability of the system. The whole thing happens so gradually and slowly that many people who are settled in subculture do not even notice, or suddenly find new opportunities. Like, for example, that finding work, renting an apartment, and just normal social things becomes easier again, so in principle more 'freedom'.

But yes, it does exactly the opposite, because once was the basic idea and the beauty of such subcultures that exactly this attitude to life and social intolerance brought a different kind of freedom, a freedom that is robbed by this social update. No, even fed to the opposite, and very few people who were once submerged in the subculture remain a hard core. They see the whole similarly contemptuous and also turn their back on the subculture and walk on.

But this core at least continues to move towards freedom.

As far back as I can remember tattooed people always fascinated me, people from remote tribes that I saw on television, books, or magazines that had stretched ears, scars, and other body modifications.

Early on I started to live in this regard. I scratched small scar patterns in my arms, started tattooing with needles and penknives. At 15, I built my first tattoo machine from a pair of Lego bricks, a pen, a sewing needle and a lot of glue. I started to make the first bigger tattoos on me, at that time all skateboard related tattoos of course. It was not all that long, and the fact that this was the time it took to get access to the Internet also helped me get the right machines a few years later. Also at that time I set up a kind of dummy company, so that I was able to acquire tattoo supplies, because at that time you could not buy such materials on eBay or anywhere. Whereupon we ordered a 50 pack of piercing needles and a few plugs, rings and labrets and later had our faces full of piercings. Several times I sat alone at home and put needles through my lip and other skin areas just to find out how different it feels in different places and what hormones the body produced in such situations. So it went on over into scars from burns, acids and with the use of a scalpel. Tattoos by hand and with a variety of traditional devices, which we copied from images, to my first small implants, which I placed on myself in the bath. Narcotics, sterilization and even basic important things like gloves were inessential at this time.

The freedom to do what I want with my body was probably my greatest attraction and the ritual experience behind it for then I knew these things only from tribes and old traditions.

And then I found BME and a new world opened up for me. For all those who do not say anything in the meantime: This was a then global community of people who lived out this kind of body modification as well and then had a platform to find each other and share their experiences. How it all got lost later is another story but the BME stands firm and with it its founder Shannon Larratt, one of the turning points in my life. Suddenly, a new world revealed itself to me of people who lived out rituals and modifications on their bodies, as I had never seen, in a new modern way. This subculture was so radical in its way that I never thought this was something that would ever be updated in the mainstream and never accepted in any way by our society. So it was the perfect world for someone like me.

During this time I had learned a lot about the matter, not only on my own body or with friends, but also just through this constant exchange of these experiences. At that time, we all still wanted to get the whole thing on, to advance in relation to the possibilities of transformations and not in relation to building a normal social acceptance.

But what happened to everything "out of the ordinary" and from my point of view is that it started with a lot of kids who discovered the whole thing and thought it was cool. It was then easy to find BME. After that there was a change and a lot of people quickly began to modify themselves in a very short time, mostly in the face or in very visible places. Since it is undeniable that internally in this sub-company is probably cooler and harder to be modified in such places. At that time I already had the feeling that there was more to it, that there were photos and proofs than the actual ritual and the personal development over all state.

Now, several years later, I can say that I was not too wrong. Many of these kids have long since dropped their modifications and undone them. But what we know about it today was never conceivable to me to that extent.

Once upon a time, I was one of those kids who had penetrated into this new world. But through my life and what I have created with it and especially with what I have undergone physically, I have probably become a fundamental part of what I despise now. I am aware that I will always be a big part of this culture, but here too I try to live for myself as far on the fringes of this society as I can.

RIP Shannon Larratt. RIP BME. RIP Bod-mod Cult.

From my point of view, there is not much left of what was once a subculture and any kind of rebellion against society is already dead before we even know what is happening to us. Personally, I don't think that in any outward fashion it is ever possible to outsmart this system and really give people the opportunity to live as a group outside of this society. What started as a rebellion was adapted through a tactical social update and nipped in the bud.

Tolerance is the death of any rebellion.

Drugs and stimulants

Now we come to the already mentioned pressure relief valves, or at least once to one of them and what lies behind it for me. As a teenager, I was dependent on certain addictive substances and drugs until I had mental confluences over a period of 3 days. This realization is now 14 years ago and has enriched and changed my life more than any other type of consciousness enhancement or realization I have ever had.

First of all, when I talk about drugs, I mean any kind of substances that cloud my consciousness, dull it and change it in a way that does not suit me personally and deprives me from the ability to be capable of what my consciousness is at full power with a clear mind. Whether legally or illegally I do not differentiate thereby. For these, in turn, are words that have been laid down by society and placed in our thoughts. Illegal means bad and legal is tolerated and in many cases even socially advocated.

Let's take alcohol.

In my opinion alcohol is the worst of all drugs, a drug that can change you depending on the dosage, from the solubility of your personality, or into another person. Alcohol is a drug that kills more people than most of the other drugs and it's a drug that probably brings the most violence, rape, murders etc. with it, far more than many illegal drugs.

Even cigarettes, how many people are dying from the use of this drug and its damage, no matter how socially accepted this drug, or how much it carries the title 'legal'.

The normality in dealing with tobacco is more than a good example. Take the tobacco industry and what is behind it. How much profit is behind it and how much evil in the world do you support with it when you smoke, how one supports the state with it, as with the alcohol and nevertheless, how many humans straight from alternative groupings, which are actually against any kind of support of the state, consume these substances?

How so? Aren't the ideals worth anything anymore? If you keep in mind how much time and money people invest in smoking and even know nothing about it. The biggest secret in the tobacco industry: 'Polonium210' and very few smokers have ever heard of it, even though they put their bodies under daily strain with this radiation, but then eat organic products and do so in a healthy and body conscious way. For me, it is incomprehensible how you can

consume a substance that you are not informed
about and that you don't really know about or
its production in third world countries and under
what conditions children and people work there.
Anyone who has been traveling in such countries
should know how it is, no matter what is said
somewhere else.

I'm convinced that if the normal smoker, once the
time and the money he accumulates annually for
it is calculated, he'd probably come to a higher
number than with one or the other hobby he has
otherwise, only with the difference that he knows
exactly about his hobbies, talks about it, informs
and educates. But let's be so good, because this
is a point that presents the blindness of many over
and over again and it makes me incredibly sad.

What do addictive substances bring us?

I had already written a
text about this topic,
which is now over 11
years old and when I
read it for the first
time yesterday, after
that long time, I
had to laugh a lot.
Not because it is so
absurd, but by how far
this basic thought is
solidified in me and
despite its own updates
and adjustments, still
relatively reflects
what I feel today.

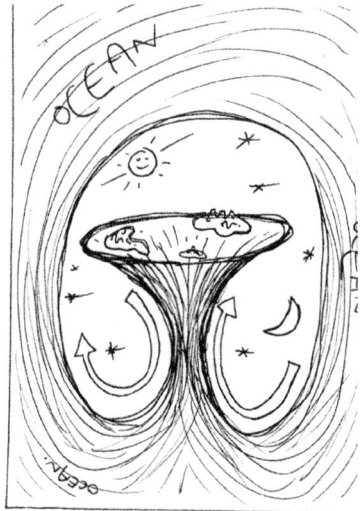

How far are drugs anchored in our society and what

do they do? I strongly believe in this so-called pressure relief valve of society. This valve, which should give the human freedom, does not let it explode in his constraints. Since the simple man is not supposed to realize how much he lives in masks and stencils and how much he is locked up, he is thrown various possibilities, small bits of freedom. And yes, drugs are a huge amount of freedom, which you throw to the man so as not to let him explode. The normal social living person is educated to how he has to function in this system so that he works Monday through Friday and then enjoys the weekend. If his entire life were monotonous and every year a repetition of the year before, while you are always looking to be socially considered. Saving money for a good car, home and other valuables that have been implanted. Well, all this life-long pressure, without interruption, would never be endured by anyone. And sooner or later, man would collapse, explode and raise questions. Just then we come to the pressure relief valve that our system has installed for this case of cases. Now we give the person some freedom and give him the impression that everything is not so bad and you have a great free life.

Drugs.

Whether legal or illegal. No matter how we label or classify certain substances

If we go on thinking, the same people probably have their fingers in the game, and changing it does nothing to my theory.

Apart from the extent to which the world is controlled, do we really believe that if the system doesn't want to have any illegal drugs on the market, would they exist?

After a week of hard work and daily adjustment how nice is it to be free after such a week at the weekend? And how far does "freeing" depend for most with the consumption of any kind of drug, especially the consumption of forbidden things and substances? Every rebel enjoys it and thinks he shows the stinky finger to the state but in reality you have both arms of the state stuck deep in the ass and you get choked on the guts.

How many go away on the weekend that involves some kind of drug use? How many use different types of drugs to go down after work in the evening? To endure everything?

How widespread is the use of alcohol and cannabis to turn off thoughts, or nicotine so you are less stressed. But doesn't it make more sense to solve the origin of it so as not to let negative thoughts and bad mood arise? Why consume a drug to cope better with the stress, even if you can just change your life so that you are not so stressed, but most likely, the normal person is distracted with much more important things than you would have time over such banalities to give thought.

Be aware at a concert, party, etc. and watch as it goes without saying that you need a beer and a cigarette and how socially accepted the whole thing is. Now I ask, how far does everything fit together?

If I listen to music on headphones during the week and dance in the city park with my eyes closed would normal people call me crazy? But if I'm drunk on the weekend it's tolerated and in some way or another, the drug gives you an excuse to behave like that. After all, behaving as one would like to behave freely wouldn't be appropriate in many situations or tolerated in the eye of society.

But that's exactly how it can convey true freedom, to behave as one feels, without having to adapt to social behavior. But true freedom is just the opposite of what the normal person should really live. As long as the cage is big enough, you do not realize that you live in captivity. As long as enough freedom is kept in mind, one will live in the belief of freedom. But how long do we want to live in a box created by others?

How is the life of someone who is completely free? I can't answer that for you because I think there is no such thing as perfect freedom in this external world. There are certainly people who have more free lives than others. But if they really have a free life or just a freer performance I can't say that. There we are again with the cage or the box. As long as I do not know about the little cage I'm locked in, I feel freer than someone living in a huge cage. The whole thing is not an easy task since both bring its advantages and disadvantages.

No drug can give you what you don't already carry in you as a human. When people say that alcohol helps them to relax, or that certain drugs help them to open one way or the other, that is mostly related to templates built by society and its manipulated ideas. Just because one then exceeds this limit with the help of a drug doesn't mean that something changes permanently. As soon as the effect of the drug wears off, one is trapped again in his old behavior patterns. A truly permanent change in consciousness definitely doesn't happen in any case. Unfortunately it is only the temporary creation of freedom in the spatial and temporal framework, which is given to you for your freedom. For example, when we get to closing time or the weekend. In my eyes, a pretty sad game that you do not even notice if you are trapped in it.

Again, it can be argued about what LSD provides as it definitely gives you things for a short time that you normally wouldn't realize but relates to things that you're definitely wearing inside and that you'll absolutely include in your life after that trip. There are probably reasons why LSD has been used so successfully in psychology and why shamans and medicine men have been using psychedelics for thousands of years. It simply gives rise to a different consciousness interaction than in the normal state and allows a completely new door to open in its subconscious. Behind these doors may lay fundamental problems. In the eye of the system, this is an undesirable problem and since man should be kept as thoughtless as possible, it is very easy to understand why LSD is classified as illegal and alcohol as legal.

The search for freedom has always been my greatest aspiration. Only what is freedom? Social dependence? Definitely not. Moments of freedom. Moments of realization. Moments of change. For my part, I fortunately realized early on how far the use of drugs keeps me from what I want to search and find in life.

Many people who persecute or know me often face the following contradiction. How can someone who publicly believes in consuming psychedelic substances have such an anti-drug attitude? But there we are again exactly in the fact that was mentioned in the first chapter. Most of what man

205

knows about things, he knows, because he got them implanted. Psychedelic substances belong to illegal substances. And all their stories and manifestations are nothing more than what you should know and believe.

LSD is not a drug. LSD is far more potent and dangerous than any drug. Because LSD does not help you turn off your thoughts and close your eyes. It does exactly the opposite. I even know what stories are there to hear about it and I agree with most of them. But just keep in mind that LSD is not a drug and should not be used like that because that's the problem. For many people, an LSD experience can be something wonderful and enriching, but also the collapse of many things. It is definitely a very strong experience that should be experienced and prepared in the right moment, in the right mood, etc. This is very important when it comes to psychedelic experiences. So it is just the opposite of how drugs are consumed. When it comes to not dealing with yourself, turning off and hiding your thoughts and then to consume LSD in such a moment is just not right and can cause serious damage.

I am convinced that you have to destroy to create something new, trade off pain for life and that you have to break yourself and destroy it completely to develop yourself as a human being. Psychedelic substances, as a prime example ayahuasca, are a nice remedy to this. However, in an environment and framework that you can catch yourself again afterwards and that you can talk to yourself and others about it and process the entire experience. This is sometimes days to weeks for months. Maybe you have experiences that will affect your life fundamentally.

You shouldn't take it easy at all and if you aren't ready then you better stay away from drugs.

I don't want to work on this topic in this book, because it's just too big a topic, about what you can do with psychedelic substances in your consciousness and change permanently but the fact is: Psychedelics are consciously expanding, not mind-limiting, regardless of the social manifestation of it. And if you are not too bad in this way of thinking, you will understand my view and if not then you will not. At any rate, my view and attitude will not cloud it. For since I had this intuition about the social context of drugs and freedom, I have no need to put my life in things that serve only to control us as a human, and especially not with socially tolerated drugs.

Social tolerance always has its downside.

Although we are actually back to free knowledge, my opinion on this subject has been shaped by unbiased experiences, to detach myself from my old ideas and to create my own. It is probably a long way to dilute your coke.

Emotions

How far can we as humans be instilled from an early age of how far we are allowed to show emotions? How wrong and insincere do we go through life with our true feelings and emotions concealed?

How many of us cry in public or show deep emotional traits in interaction with their environment? From an early age we are told that smiling is something good and crying is not but how far are all kinds of feelings related? How far are we able to socially solve ourselves so that we cry when we feel like this, no matter where we are and who is around us? No longer having the urge to pull it together.

I am a very emotional person, or let's just say that I have become a very emotional person. This confronted me with many situations like this in my life. To experience how the normal person just doesn't understand that someone is sitting there crying and showing deep emotions, no matter what happens around him.

The whole thing is strongly related to the social norms and morality that we are pressed into, in which normal-human needs are disregarded.

Many of the topics in this book are attributed to a chapter, because by and large, most of the issues raised here are related anyway, whether they're thoughts, society, emotions and other topics. Everything is a total package and influenced and guided by each other.

Sexism is a good example of this. How hard do women and men adjust to be viewed? It is for many a huge taboo break only to fart in front of your partner or to go to the toilet together. But why are we so messed up? Do most people see this as messing up and working on it? Or is it usually just accepted, although you find it positive or not? It simply is not questioned as it is deeply rooted in our morality?

It was apparently taught to us at some point what is "normal" and what you have to do in this regard.

It all starts at a very early age, while children are completely free and uninhibited about gender distribution; most parents start to burden them with their parental influence and their own lives. Why are girls dressed pink and boys, blue, just to name a very small example? And yes, even if we avoid this as a parent, our children are still exposed to society and quickly learn what it means to be a girl or to be a boy and how to behave and show.

Why, for example, are there make-up sets for little girls? This only shows how early women are pressed into this rail. It's not much different with the boys. How soon does this image of the "Strong Man" begin to take shape in the heads of the children? A real man doesn't cry because he is brave and strong. Just one example of many and this picture is not just put in the heads of men but just the other way around with everything.

Once viewed from the male side, how did a real man behave? What does it mean to be a man in the eye of society? Our entire gender concept is still as firmly rooted in us as it used to be. Of course, many things have changed over the last few decades and there is no comparison to what it was like a hundred years ago, or how it still is today in many countries, tribes and cultures, nevertheless the sexual influence is omnipresent.

Society tells us through media, television etc. how a pretty woman looks and nearly every woman tries to fit within this picture using make-up, clothes and so on and everything just to fit into the ideal 'pretty woman' picture. But how far do we question this overall picture? How far does this even correspond to the idea of the man? Because the man is not as influenced by sexism as the woman? Does the normal man have this idea at all, or is it nothing but an idea that is just as influenced? This bilateral gender struggle is putting up pressure on both sides and that starts early. Why are there high heels for little children or make-up sets? These ideal concepts we should carry within us, but why? It is another step to stop man from seeing the world more openly, another template that holds us and tells us that when we get this ideal image or achieve something we have achieved something.

If we live long in our whole life, it is not easy for us to let go of it. I myself have started letting go of my gender over the past few years, or at least play around with it a bit.Since I was well aware of this gender-related behavior, it was and still is very hard to see how you yourself are. When I first wore a women's skirt in public I felt so silly and it's really just a piece of clothing. But even realizing how deeply this gender behavior is rooted in one is a blatant experience. And above all, the reaction of other same-sex people is definitely more than exciting. As if one is not only attacking his own masculinity but the entire male species. In any case, funny and one thing I can say, the entire transsexual men who live their lives as women have a hundred times more balls than most men in our society. Because that is a big step out of the normality of the system and to put your own instinctive emotional behavior on what you should actually do.

I no longer see myself as a man but not as a woman either. I see myself more as someone who is free to choose what he feels like. I also usually wear a mix of women's clothing and men's clothing. Whether it has anything to do with this for myself, the convenience or just because I like it is hard to say. I would say that everything is true and you, like this outer shell, like to adapt to how you feel inside. At least you should do that and

210

not the other way around. Why should I feel like a man just because I'm in a male body?

Not only do I relate this behavior to our society, but it is also rooted and anchored in our subcultures. Although there is a different concept of beauty there, still masks and stencils in which most are trapped.

Those who don't adapt are usually excluded very quickly or even lose their place within this grouping because there are no really completely free and unprejudiced life forms in which people live together.

To come back to emotions.

How beautiful are true and free emotions? How good does it feel to really release one's emotions, whether positive or negative? I would say emotions are the strongest bodily expression with which you can externally convey what you really feel in your mind. Unfortunately society tells us how we should act as human beings, or how we behave as a man and how we behave as a woman, to really break it out and accept that this is just a delusion that is created socially to distract us from the truth.

True feelings are dangerous. If you show that you are unhappy you will quickly be labeled as depressed or ill. Which normal human is already crying in public or showing deep human emotions to a degree that is simply abnormal to normal people?

To continue on the topic of emotions, I wrote a text a few months ago about one of my deepest emotions; the feeling of loneliness that I carry because the external world is so strange to me. And I've been struggling for a long time to publish the text. I recently had a deep emotional trip and that feeling and realization of loneliness was as strong as ever. I also realized how weak it is to be completely free to express my emotions and not to publish this text, although it is also an emotion that guides me strongly in my life. To go one step further and break a big limit for myself, I published it with a photo where I cry.

For me personally that was one of the strongest decisions of my life. Rather than live in the masquerade, as everyone makes the biggest thoughts on how he looks in pictures and appears happy and satisfied and how a life is played, which is often the opposite of the mirror of his soul, especially in this day and age when many people live more on the Internet or value this projection more than their true life.

Some people go so far as to describe me as a pussy and a crying girl but it doesn't matter to me since these are only people who have been implanted with this reality. To find true freedom, to let go of these social norms and to show how freely one feels, can be a beautiful thing and more liberating than carrying it with oneself for years.

Now we come to the text I just talked about. Since I find it a very important topic and it was difficult for me for a long time to really be aware of it. What does it mean to be different? Or, What is "different"? I am aware that every person is somehow different. We live in other cultures, countries and realities. And every human being is somehow different, apart from the external variances. That's not even what I'm talking about, not just the character traits or the like, I'm talking about the inner feeling, the feeling of being different than the majority of society, the feeling that doesn't allow you to adapt.

These days it feels like everyone is trying to be different, especially in subcultures and other lifestyles. Everyone wants to be special, different and somehow unique. Everyone thinks it's cool to be different. But what does that actually mean, or what impact does it have on his life when he is really different? What does it mean to be "different"? And I'm not talking about externally; I'm talking about the state of consciousness. From an early age I felt different and could never adapt, neither in school, nor in society, or later in any subcultures.

At some point, I just took that and anchored it in my mind. Changing my body outwardly was just another step in processing or adapting to this whole process to adapt my body to my soul, so to speak.

Meanwhile, I see the whole thing a little differently. I have accepted that I am not different, but that my imagination and my life are normal. Everything else is different and abnormal. The normal "normal" does not exist anymore and probably never will. But when you realize this reality, you quickly realize that there are few normal people in the world, in the sense that is normal for me, and with my idea of life.

Sometimes I wonder what it would be like to be "normal", as in socially normal, and to accept life as it is; within all the masks and stencils we are supposed to live in, a simple life. Swim. Consequences. To be guided.

But every time it came to authoritarian stuff or other adaptive social features, I just could not adapt. And one day I just gave up completely and accepted it as it is.

One thing I can say, it's not an easy life. It's not cool to be different and it's a lonely, long road, where you find very few people, situations and things that you can identify with. There are only a few people that you see as normal and that you can approach and the longer you live the more extreme the whole thing gets, the more you exclude yourself. You start to hate the world and its environment more, including all humanity and their beliefs. Normal people blindly run through life. Yes, there is a lot of hate, and you really start to appreciate only a few things, things that are very important to you and that you are very close to at heart. Things that are bigger than you would ever have dreamed. But surrounded by hate and loneliness.

I live in a world of billions of people and I cannot identify with anyone, individuals, cultures, religions, belief systems or anything else. I did not choose this feeling and this life, but I accepted it for myself. I have accepted that the world in which I live is another, one with few people and little earthly things that really bring me fulfillment. The result is that you isolate yourself more and more from the world. You move into nowhere, avoiding cities or any kind of events or gatherings of people. Almost afraid to go into the normal world and hide from society. At the same time my outer shell adapts to the situation and embodies my inner feelings more and more.

I'm not worried anymore if I'm different or if my environment looks different to me, or whether it's cool or not. In myself I feel the loneliness that

214

comes with it when you are different, as if you are the only normal person in his world.

I feel normal, in such an abnormal world in which we live.

In my imagination there is simply no functioning social system. Because if everyone were really different, if everyone really was free in their own way, then the individual lives would be so fundamentally different that a human interaction would no longer be possible. Perhaps even the level of social coexistence or the pressure to adapt would no longer exist and a real interaction would no longer be necessary, at least in a forced way. Say, any interaction would be completely free and casual.

That in turn could work but would definitely not be any form of society in itself anymore.

ADDENDUM

The times in which I wrote the rough draft of this book were some of the hardest and deepest in my life from my emotional point of view. This was due to external circumstances plus the fact of finally writing down everything that has guided me in my life and most likely will continue to guide me in some way. Let's call it self-reflection on a large scale. And only after about 2 years, I look back on this time and I can just laugh about what state of mind I was in when I decided to write a book. Yes, sometimes you have to fall and sometimes really hard.

I still believe that there is no such thing as "bad experiences" in life. Everything that happens redeems itself in the future as a valued experience. It is often these rather negative experiences that spur us on to give even more. They grant us incentive to make more of our lives. They give us the kick in our asses we needed. If everything were perfect or, let's say, satisfying, we'd rarely be able to change it even if the final outcome were better than before. We'd probably end up being in fear again or simply falling back in the habit of not effecting change. Either way, the downtimes of my life were very chaotic, because I just let everything run together in that chaos, consciously or unconsciously. In those moments, I would say it just happens. But objectively and from a temporal distance, I have to say that it is up to me to make the best of the big decisions in front of me during these deep times.

How deep can I fall if I have already buried myself in the ground?

Because even my box is constantly changing and another big reason I wanted to write this book is so I can read my point of view for myself. I hope that I can break away from my ego later on and read my book completely free, impartial and objectively and just think about it myself. Confronting yourself in your head with your thoughts is a nice thing. But reading it in a book from a neutral point of view is another matter. Presently, I do not know that yet, as this is my first experience of this kind and I'd like to let a few months pass in order to have that distance to look at myself in a completely new and objective way. I believe this will change my box and my own reality a lot and one should question oneself and question how everything else in the world is. Because nothing is as it seems and maybe not even your own reality.

I like to joke with everything and everyone. I try not to take anything too seriously and accept things as they are. I like to call the whole thing "The law of poops".

It is what it is. When you move a stone, a stone moves, nothing more and nothing less because it is exactly what you do and nothing more, nothing less. Yes, it is stupid and idiotic, true and unassailable. Nevertheless, I experience it from pure free knowledge and not from what is told to me.

Do not take life too seriously otherwise it will just be too serious.

I can only repeat that I am not a spiritual man, not a Shaman, not an esoteric, or an ultra spiritual hippie. I decided a long time ago that I did not want to wait for any spiritual experience that might change my life. I live in the "here and now" and my actions, my doing, my creation, and my thoughts are what fill and guide me.

To fart loudly and laugh about it brings me much more happiness and joy than doing two hours of yoga in the morning and waiting for enlightenment. I try to let go of adulthood more and more and take myself even less seriously every day.

So it was a very emotional but also touching experience of my life, at any rate, to write down deep trains of thought in this way and be somehow working it out for the first time.

Many things here may not make too much sense. So it is even better, that I do not take myself too seriously and laugh about it rather than cry.

The way I live my life may seem stupid or ill considered to others. But somewhere deep in this confusion, which I call "my ego", it is completely logical and thoughtful and the most natural in my world to live the way I do. It feels right and if not, then there is no reason for me to do anything at all.

Because everyone is influenced by their thoughts and actions every day and thus lives in their own box, within their own template and own point of view. To break away from this, over and over again is what personally brings me the most development and freedom in the external world.

Because what would life be with a standstill? If a seed that is not planted and watered, it is a box that never changes. Leave the box and burn it down. After all, every human being has a choice of how they live, even if they may not yet know or admit it. We have this one life on earth completely in our hands, in which we can make and create, we can only determine it once, and only if we do what our heart tells us.

How far do we go when terrain is uneven and rocky? When it goes up and down, tree trunks and debris are in the way and strong windstorms are against us. Take off your shoes, strap on a heavy, stone-filled backpack and walk the path. If you have the belief that there is no longer a goal, it does not matter how far you go. Only the steps are of importance. So watch where you're going.

One meter of your path can mean much more than 167,320,671 km to where you do not want to be. If the uncertainty becomes certain, hasn't one part of the peace of mind been found? Are there no more fulfillments than to live in uncertainty, to live in dreams and thoughts, and then you have the opportunity to make them your reality.

Some things take longer than others. It took me 10 years to write this book. Another 2 years until I had overwritten it and have it halfway make sense. I'm glad I did it and it will not be my last book. But I'm sad that it took me 10 years to do it because most likely it would have changed my box much earlier in a new way and who knows where I would be today then?

There is only "too late" on this earth when the countdown catches up. But if you are aware of it and consciously decide, then nothing will happen too late in your life. Or, in this case, too late means never.

Because life is transient and so are the possibilities it brings.

Credits & Pictures

Cover: Lily Lu. Picture: Esra Sam

Contentpage Picture: Carnivore Pictures

P23, 159, 162 : Psyland archives.

P28: Top left + bottom right: Psyland archive. Top right: Thai guy. Bottom left: Kor.

P70: Top left and bottom: Psyland archive. Top right: Pipeshots.

P72: Top left: Anuskatzz. Top right: Lily. Bottom: Pipeshots.

P117: Top: Visavajra. Bottom: Lily.

P118: Top left: Morle. Top right: Psyland archives. Bottom: Flying Swastika.

P168: Top left: Lily, Top right: Carnivore Pictures. Bottom: Vanessa Steffen.

Credits: Selfportrait (Third dimension Project)

About the Author: Ash Fyr. Picture: Pipeshots and Selfportrait

All drawings: Lily Lu

Words from the translater: Niels Nijim. Picture: Micha

Advice and German correction: "Dorsch" Meltem Meddur

English translation, Photoshop & grafic help: Niels Nijim

English correction: Rita Amanita

Layout: Eswari Kamireddy

Tempe of inspiration: Psyland 25

ABOUT THE AUTHOR

Lily Lu is a true visionary filmmaker, a modern shamanic philosopher of life, formerly Little Swastika, as a tattooist she pushed boundaries with groundbreaking tattooing techniques including the Love Tattoo over 4 backs and then the 3rd Dimension Project the worlds biggest tattoo over 10 backs.

Lily Lu's previous persona Little Swastika quit tattooing in 2019 to dedicate herself to filmmaking. Her unique tattooing style is known worldwide and it is a progression of the tattoo artform. Her large back pieces, body suits and group projects are notoriously recogniseable in the tattoo world.

Born in 1986, she is an artist from Southern Germany. She spent most of her life as a male and now lives life as a female. Just as she has transformed art and tattooing so she has herself, turning inward to confront her own male ego and blossoming with Love, turning normal societies ideas on their head and defining her own gender.

Lily Lu is a creator, an artist, an independent filmmaker, an author and the builder of her own world. Her filmmaking is powerful and visionary, reflecting her eclectic style that is deeply rooted in Tengen at a place called "Psyland 25" more than a tattoo studio, more like an alternative playground for adults and an empire. She calls this her modern "temple" and it is by far her biggest masterpiece of creative art.

She is a lover of life and someone who believes in nothing. For her life is about love, passion and doing impossible things, crossing borders and doing what is considered by some as extreme. For her flesh hook body suspension, experimenting with psychadelics, extreme body modification, eyeball tattooing, BDSM, polyamory, fetishism and alternative porn are an everyday part of her alternative subculture she calls life. She loves shamanic rituals, philosophical thought and everything that has touched her heart and mind. Her love is deeply expressed and through the use of her hands she has built up her home 'Psyland 25' and manifested it as her biggest dream.

Her vision as a filmmaker is to document the beauty of true alternative lifestyle, to show what is behind the surface, the real raw truth, the beauty and the love within her and others in her world.

Lily Lu has been prolifically producing and conveying her documented vision through short films, small documentaries on her YouTube channels, more kinky films for Dirty Dreaz and aims to breakthrough into feature films in the future.

Lily Lu has been filmmaking for many years as a part of her Dirty Dreaz Project and winning film awards for her raw and edgy alternative xxx films.

She has travelled the world and has been heavily influenced by Asian Tibetan art and writing, developing her own sanscrit style called Psyscrit, heavily represented in her art style of tattooing and painting.

She has published multiple art books, a childrens fiction book. She has also been interviewed and published in the international press all over the world.

She shares her life with her beautiful wife and female model Anuskatzz and her daughter Maya.

2008

2019

WHY AM I HERE?

A brief story from the translator

I remember very clearly my first experience of seeing a Little Swastika tattoo. I couldn't turn my eyes from the screen back in 2010. I think it was the 4-back-piece with the word "LOVE" tattooed across four backs as one art piece. Back then I'd been researching the swastika and the meaning aside from the "nazi-cliché". I already learned a lot about it when suddenly Marc appeared on my Google-search screen, showing his hands with his pretty much freshly cut off ring finger tips. I tried to wrap my head around the motives that this fellow might have had for doing this. Even though he explained it roughly, it was mysterious to me. What came to my mind, when I read all these weird and sometimes hateful comments under the picture that he had posted on Facebook was deep respect for this person who I didn`t know. Yet, I found out more and more over the next two years but never had the guts to even ask for an appointment for a tattoo, as I was certain of tow things; a) This shit surely hurts like hell and b) I guess, I cannot afford this! The distance set aside, as I live on the other end of the country. When I finally wrote that mail and asked for a 'smaller' tattoo, the answer went something like this: "No small tattoos! A backpiece is the minimum" and the cost of the three sessions needed? Well, it exceeded my budget by far, so I discarded the idea but asked his fellow artists that work with him at Psyland soon after.

I made my first appointment for covering up my arm

233

with Manu, one of Little Swastikas apprentices on my fortieth birthday. Two weeks later, my sixteen-year-old daughter got diagnosed with a super-rare form of cancer. A grapefruit sized sarcoma had wrapped around one of her ovaries and needed to be removed in an emergency operation. Chemotherapy followed and due to miscalculations by the doctors, she fell into a coma for four weeks in which time she was clinically dead twice. It was during that time when I was supposed to travel through the country to have my first session with Manu. My daughters mum and I were debating whether it was a good idea for me to go. In the end, I went to that session and secretly turned it into a kind of protection ritual for my daughter. Secret meaning that I didn't tell Manu about my, I admit it, naive visualization of him pulling the cancer out of my daughters body (the ink in the cup) through his tattoo-gun and injecting it into my skin. It was only at our third session on my arm that I told him. Needless to say he was pretty much shocked about my confession.

Almost a year had passed when finally Marc and I made a barter-deal so he could tattoo me without having this stupid thing called "money" involved. I followed Little Swastika's Facebook profile and every now and then I made comments, not only ironic ones about his denglish ("D" for Deutsch) but also in response to whatever was the actual subject of his post. After all, I then had and still do have a great respect for this man. After some private messaging back and forth I offered my help to translate the book of which he stated briefly on Facebook that he'd been "working on for quite a while". Marc decided that I "wouldn't be the worst" to do the job. We agreed to this deal on the June 21, 2016. Later in the evening of that *day my daughter died. Peacefully, thanks to modern palliative medicine and our loving care at home.*

Obviously it took a while until Marc had all the parts of his book ready to be translated and for me to "get my shit together", which I guess I never fully will, but that is not really the subject here. In early 2017, I collected the parts that were written by Marc and by all means, I just couldn't get into it. I just couldn't wrap my head around these deep and thoughtful words that this guy has written down. They just didn't make any sense to me. It was not until we had a brief Skype session where he told me that his sole motive was to simply write a book. Apart from the 2014 video documentary by Claudio Marino "Ink, Blood and Spirit", which was on Vimeo, this was the first time I'd heard him speaking. I should add that I'm a musician and, due to that, a very phonetic person. From that day on, I could enter the matter a little better and briefly started lecturing and then translating this book.

Because I knew that Marc is very much into rituals, we chose our first date to work on my backpiece on the same date we fixed our barter, only two years later. It was the second angelversary of my daughter, Pain against pain. For some reason, I could sense, that I would be in good hands and that this, other then her first angelversary, which was a dreadful experience, would help me to move on in my grief process more than any pill, herb or psychological bla bla. I call it the "metamorphosis samurai", which is the first chorus line from the "Red Hot Chili Peppers" song, 'Dreams of a Samurai', which I love very much and which is, in a way, very much connected to my daughter's passing.

235

So I went to Psyland for a third time. I never met Marc, even when I had the first two sessions with Manu in the gallery and the third session on my arm was done in a town near my place up in Northern Germany. The day before our session at Psyland we had a barbecue in the garden, and had some beautiful talks. I knew it was the right thing to do, spending this day in the way I did.

The tattoo-session itself was both awful and enlightening. Horribly beautiful and, believe it or not, refreshing in a way. I knew already that for Marc skin is just a canvas and he doesn't give a shit how much the people he's tattooing are suffering or not. "If you're moaning or crying or yelling too loud, I just crank the music up more so I can`t hear you anymore". The ink has to get into skin and that is that. But Marc is quick. We were done with the first third of my back on that day. I couldn't tell how long it took him. It could have been two hours or twelve, but I guess not too long, three hours maybe. These three hours felt like a little eternity in my personal hell, as well as a little drop of time in Psyland-heaven. I cried a lot that day. I laughed a lot that day. And I felt love. Love for this man who was willingly spending an awfully tagged day with me and who helped me to make it a little less awful but instead gave me pieces of my dignity back, who dealt pain for pain with me. And, for some reason that might be hard to grasp, I felt loved. Trying to put this into words is not an easy task but what is? Especially when it comes to love. You either love or you don't. I decided to love. I find it easier.

Today, five months after that first session with Marc, I had my second and third session and being *here in Psyland feels like being at home away from home with a bunch of sweet weirdoes around me. With a lot of blood, sweat and tears (yes, I cried today, too!) and a lot of "Why am I here? Why am I doing this?" in my head. Oh and with "sweet weirdoes" I honestly mean some of the most beautiful, friendly, lovely, loving, caring and honest people I've ever met in my entire life, who let me be part of their 16:12 family and who made me sane with the insanity of this place and the rituals we went through. I will forever be grateful for this until I leave this physical shell one day and until then, I will wear my samurai shield with pride, which will be complete by tomorrow. Thank you so much for this, Marc.*

Love,
Niels (November 2018)

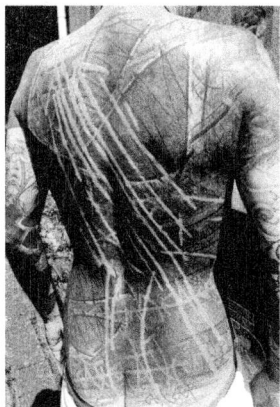

Printed in Great Britain
by Amazon